THE SUCCESSFUL FRANCHISE

THE SUCCESSFUL FRANCHISE
A Working Strategy

Golden Square Services Limited

Gower

This edition published in 1985 by Gower Publishing Company Limited, Gower House, Croft Road, Aldershot, Hants GU11 3HR, England.

Published in 1984 by Golden Square Services Limited, a firm of independent investment and financial planning consult-ants, of 84, Church Street, Old Town, Eastbourne, East Sussex BN21 1QJ (tel. (0323) 645151).

British Library Cataloguing in Publication Data

The successful franchise : a working strategy.
1. Franchises (Retail trade) — Great Britain
I. Golden Square Services
658.8'708'0941   HF5429.235.G7

ISBN 0-566-02584-1

Typeset by Graphic Studios (Southern) Ltd, Godalming, Surrey.
Printed in Great Britain by Billing & Sons Limited, Worcester.

Contents

This is no ordinary book. Although it can be read as you would any other book that is not the best way of making the most of the layout and design incorporated in The Successful Franchise.

The book is divided into sections. The early sections deal with the broad picture and the principles involved. The later sections look at more specialised areas of concern.

The principal text is set out with wide margins for your notes. You may make notes as you read, in the margin next to the relevant text – remember this is no ordinary book so do not hesitate to write in it. Also in these principal sections you will find frequent side headings. These are intended to help you scan the text quickly. Add more headings of your own to aid this process.

The checklists accompanying each section provide an opportunity for analysing your own particular situation.

The case-histories illustrate how theory can translate into practice in real life situations.

A directory of useful names and addresses is provided at the end of the book.

Section 1

Buying a blueprint for success

What are you letting yourself in for when you purchase a franchise? This section explains why business format franchising has become so successful and the main advantages and disadvantages of franchising as a way of starting a business. It also shows how to distinguish between this form of franchising and other forms that may be offered. The checklist will help you decide whether the franchises you have your eye on meet the criteria for a genuine business format franchise.

Definition **Franchisor:– The person or company who owns a business idea, name or process and who grants a licence for the use of that name, idea or process to a FRANCHISEE.**

Franchising is a big business made up of a lot of successful little guys. In the United States franchising accounts for one-third of all retail sales. While the figure for the UK is much lower, that simply goes to show the vast potential still to be exploited from franchised sales.

Look at these facts concerning franchising in the United States:

● In all there are about 250,000 franchisees in the US.

1

Among these are

● Some 75,000 retail outlets

● Some 70,000 restaurants

● Over 16,000 firms in the home improvement, maintenance and cleaning fields.

Franchising in the UK is rapidly following the same pattern, with thousands of independent minded people taking advantage of the growing number and variety of franchises on offer each year. As a result, over the past four years the number of franchise outlets in the UK has doubled.

What makes franchising so attractive?

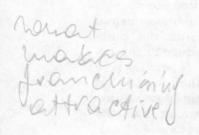

For a start, the fact that it *works.* The annual sales turnover of the 40 or so franchisors who are members of the British Franchise Association is growing at 16% per annum – much faster than the British economy as a whole. As most franchises rely for their sales turnover primarily on the increased turnover of their franchisees, the formula must be working.

Another attraction is that franchising is, by and large, a much safer bet than starting a completely independent business from scratch. The franchisor should have been through all the learning problems and expensive mistakes inherent in starting up a new business. He is in effect selling you the experience to avoid them. That is one of the main reasons why franchise businesses have a much better survival rate than new small businesses in general. Indeed, your franchise has almost 2½ times greater a chance of becoming a success than the average new business.

That is not to say that franchising is a totally safe bet. Some people are simply not suited to this kind of business (we will help you decide just how well you are suited to it in section two). And, because large scale franchising is still a relatively new phenomenon in the UK, there are pitfalls for the unwary.

Not all franchises are the golden opportunity they seem, and the legal protections for the franchisee are inadequate. So it is very important to be able to evaluate the claims made by franchisors and to understand exactly what you are signing up for.

The third factor that makes franchising so attractive is that it is a half-way house between total independence and working for someone else. For anyone used all his or her life to working in a large firm the transition to full independence can be quite traumatic. Franchising is a comfortable in-between step which you can use to gain the experience and confidence in running a small business you may need to branch out on your own.

Nonetheless, many people, having tried franchising, stick with it permanently, in some cases building up lucrative chains of franchised outlets. For example, Richard Carr, managing director of Allied Restaurants, is still in his early 20s. He started off with a single Wimpy restaurant in Bournemouth in 1981. Although trade was disappointing at first, both he and Wimpy persevered with promotion campaigns in the town and were rewarded with rapid growth in business. In 1983 the Bournemouth restaurant won Wimpy's top store award and Carr had expanded his Wimpy chain to six outlets.

Let's look now at what franchising is and where it came from.

A short history of franchising

Franchising
began with the
tied pub

Franchising has become so much part of the American way of life that the Americans have begun to claim they invented the idea. This is not the case. It goes back to the middle ages – some even say to the Romans. But from the point of view of most readers its most familiar form goes back to 150 years ago, to the tied pub.

When the urban population started to expand, so did the market of thirsty workers. The problem for the breweries was: how could they get to them without starting hundreds of pubs on their own and getting stuck with all the management problems that this entailed? The answer was to offer premises at a reduced rent to licensees, provided that they undertook to get their supplies from the brewer. That, of course, put the licensee somewhat at the mercy of the supplier as far as price and quality were concerned. On the other hand, ultimately both their interests were the same. If the product, the price and the service were poor, customers would go elsewhere and they would both be losers.

That is still the basic principle of *business format franchising.*

With time, however, the term franchising has come to be applied to a number of activities which don't fit the description of business format franchising at all. Unfortunately, it would be quite legal for an advertiser to describe these as a franchise, even though they may not have anything like the same value as the business format franchise. Most of these forms of franchise are described later in this section, where you will find a chart which will help you identify these kinds of franchise.

Our concern, however, is with business format franchising, which we will refer to from here on as simply franchising.

Because there is so little legislation about franchising, there is no legal definition of it either. The British Franchise Association – a body to which most, but not all reputable franchisors belong – has developed a definition of its own, but rather than bother with legal terminology, let's look and see what it means for practical purposes.

What a business format franchise is

● It is a method of distribution or marketing in which a company (the franchisor) grants a contract to an individual or another company (the franchisee) the right to carry on a business in a prescribed way in a particular territory for a specified period.

● It is a service, like instant printing, or a retail activity, like a speciality shop with a product and a method of operating that has been demonstrably tried and found to work; preferably over a period of time and in circumstances similar to those which the franchisee is in. It often also has characteristics which are claimed to be unique – e.g. a special recipe like the sauce in Kentucky Fried Chicken.

● The franchisor provides a market survey of the territory which substantiates his claims in regard to income and profit projections.

● The method of operating is set out in a manual which covers everything from the "unique" ingredients or properties of the franchised product to accounting procedures or the design of fixtures, fittings and graphics to be employed in the franchise.

● The franchisor provides promotional back-up plus training and trouble shooting services to the franchisee. He may also help him (or her) get the business off the ground, in the case of some of the more sophisticated and expensive franchises, by helping him to get planning permission, raise finance, negotiate leases and so on.

● The franchisee may have to buy supplies or equipment from sources nominated by the franchisor.

● The franchisee has to pay an initial fee and a continuing royalty to the franchisor in exchange for the "blueprint" plus the other services described in the contract.

● Though the franchisor exercises considerable control over the operation of the franchise, the business itself belongs to the franchisee. He remains free to sell it and retain the profit, though the franchisor may either ask for first refusal if he wishes to sell, or the right to approve another purchaser, or both. The right to sell the franchise is a characteristic distinguishing business format franchising from other kinds.

The pros and cons of franchising

Like any other form of business, there are advantages and disadvantages to franchising, as summarised below:

Plus points

Bulk buying power
1. The bulk buying power of the franchisor often means that you can obtain supplies at a much lower cost than as an independent operator.

Planning permission
2. Handling complex planning and building applications can be a time consuming chore on your own; the franchisor will normally have specialist staff to help you through the planning jungle.

Market studies
3. Detailed studies of local markets can greatly improve your chances of success. Your franchisor will normally be able to provide these or help you do them.

National advertising
4. The chain of franchised outlets together can fund a much greater advertising and promotional campaign than you could ever afford on your own. Faced with a national name they have heard of and a local name they have not heard of, most customers will plump for what they know.

Shorter learning curve
5. Every new business has a "learning curve" when you make simple, sometimes fatal mistakes – the product isn't quite right, your prices are slightly too high or too low, you would have done better if you'd had more storage space or whatever. Because the franchise has been tried and tested by the franchisor, and perhaps other franchisees before you, you eliminate at least the rougher bends in the learning curve.

Lower capital outlay
6. In most cases the capital outlay is lower than if you started from scratch, though some established franchises can be very expensive. Wimpy states that the required capital investment in equipment, mechanical services and shop-fitting runs to "at least £170,000". However you can

eliminate the factors of initial waste and mistakes that commonly account for at least 25% of the start-up cost.

Design aid

7. Design and layout of premises and the presentation of product and services can make or mar a new business, especially something like a shop or restaurant. Interior designers can cost the earth. The franchisor already has a specification in the blueprint, so ideally all you have to find are tradesmen who can follow instructions.

Help when unwell

8. Though you are largely on your own, the most established and well-known franchisors at least have trouble shooting headquarters staff who can rally round in an emergency – for instance if you fall ill. It's in their interest as well as yours that you should be successful, not only because it maintains their royalty income, but because one franchise which gets into difficulties can reflect badly on all the others.

past back-up

Minus points

You pay regardless

1. A royalty has to be paid, usually monthly and based on turnover, to the franchisor. Franchisees quite often come to regard this as a sore point, particularly if they feel that the franchisor has pulled less than his weight in building up the business. Irrespective of this, you have to pay what the contract says you must.

Turnover v profit

2. A royalty based on turnover can mean that the franchisor can push you into promotional ventures that increase turnover without increasing profitability.

Will I have continued support?

3. The successful operation of the franchise depends very much on the continued support of the franchisor. This is not invariably forthcoming. The spirit, as well as the letter of the contract, is important, but where the spirit is not willing it is very difficult to coerce it by legal means.

The franchisor may go bust

4. There is virtually no protection to the franchisee in cases where the franchisor runs into financial difficulties and is unable to fulfil his obligations.

Can I buy cheapest?

5. Where the franchisee is obliged to obtain goods and services from the franchisor, these may not be at competitive rates compared to other possible sources.

Will my freedom be limited?

6. The essence of the franchise operation is in the blueprint and that makes for almost total uniformity – franchising is a cloning exercise. The franchisor, in fact, has a great deal of control over how the place looks, or when it opens, or how much it charges, but also what trading activities may or may not be carried on there. The franchisee, for instance, may see opportunities, which the franchisor can prevent him from taking. Franchising, therefore, is not always an activity to be recommended to the aggressively entrepreneurial or independent-minded.

Can I sell the business later?

7. The franchisee does not have total control over the disposal of the business. The purchaser has to be approved by the franchisor – not unreasonably, because it is essential from his point of view that all outlets are in competent and approved hands. It is also a peculiarity of franchising that the good-will remains the possession of the franchisor, whereas the franchisee often feels that the goodwill has been built up at least partially by his efforts. However, the real value of goodwill has increasingly been challenged in recent years – for instance the *Daily Telegraph* Guide to Buying a Shop heads that section "Goodwill and the Rubbish People Talk About It"! Goodwill, the author says in effect, is only the difference between what you might get for the assets at best and their break-up value. What is more to the point in the case of a franchise, is that any equipment you have bought to specifications laid down by the franchisor may not be saleable on the open market, so the franchisor can in any case dictate what the goodwill value of the business is. This does not, however, mean that if you succeed in selling equipment at a good price the franchisor is entitled to take the profit.

Other forms of franchising

Exclusive right
to trade

One very familiar form of franchising is the *exclusive right to trade* in a particular product or service over a particular territory. For example, the British Airports Authority franchises firms to hold the catering and other trading concessions at their airports. Similarly, motorway cafés have been franchised by the government to firms like Granada or Trust House Forte. The basis of such franchises is that the franchisee pays a royalty, usually based on turnover, to the franchisor and undertakes to observe a specification of conduct and performance laid down by him – agreeing for instance, to stay open all hours, including those during which operations are probably going to be unprofitable.

This form of franchising may well grow because it accords with the government's policy of privatisation; for instance a number of local authorities have granted waste collection franchises to private firms; the proviso being that they should offer a service at least as good as that which had been provided by the council's own staff for a sum based on a competitive tender. There has also been talk of franchising catering on British Rail. This form of franchising resembles the business format variety in that the franchisor:

● Grants a concession in an exclusive territory for a stated period of time

● Gets a fee and/or a royalty

● Lays down performance standards.

However, the franchisor does not offer a particular method of operating, as is the case with business format franchising where the franchisee has to work out for himself the best way to run the business.

Distributorship
or agency

Another form of trading for which the term franchise is often used is a *distributorship*, for instance for a make of car or type of computer. This is sometimes referred to as an *agency*, but there is an important legal difference between them. The words or deeds by which an agent represents a product or service are binding on the company he represents, as if they were employer and employee, irrespective of their actual relationship. A distributor is quite independent, though in other respects his transactions with a third party are exactly like those of an agent. Commonly, his relationship with his principal would embrace, in addition to an exclusive territory concession:

● an undertaking to hold a required level of stock.

● an agreement to maintain the premises in a way that would reflect favourably on the principal's product or service.

● the supply of promotional material by the supplying company, plus back-up services like the training of staff, partial, or total funding of advertising for the product, and mention of the agent or distributor in the supplier's promotional literature, where appropriate.

Celebrity name or registered trade mark

Celebrity name franchising first became associated with "endorsements" by film stars – there is, for instance, a famous forties poster of Ronald Reagan commending the virtues of the American cigarette "Lucky Strike" – and moved on to branded goods, particularly in sport. Fred Perry shirts were probably the first British example and there is now a growing practice to franchise designer marques: Calvin Klein jeans or Mary Quant lipstick. For the use of a famous name the manufacturer pays a royalty. The same principle applies to the use of registered trademarks or patent. This kind of franchising is further removed from the variety we are talking about, except that one of its characteristics is:

● the uniform use of a name which is promoted in the expectation that it will be recognisable to customers.

Celebrity names, however, may be only vaguely associated with an image or a lifestyle – not necessarily with the performance of the product. They sell the sizzle, not the steak, while business format franchising sells both.

Pyramid selling

After this we start to sail in murkier waters. One of the problems of franchising is that there has been very little legislation about it. There is however one field where the law has stepped in and that is in the version, or perversion of franchising known as "pyramid selling". In pyramid selling there is still a product involved, but this is secondary to the main objective which is to sell a "distributorship" for it. The franchisee is given a certain territory and is rewarded for recruiting distributors, who are also persuaded to invest heavily in the franchisor's product as "opening stock". They become, in effect, sub-franchisees, and are lured by rosy projections on a product that, certainly in the sixties when pyramid selling reached scandal proportions, was often not viable. Pyramid selling was prohibited in the 1973 Fair Trading Act, but it occasionally rears its ugly head in other guises which stay just inside the legal fence. A recent franchise advertisement in a national newspaper, for instance, invited applicants to become "regional consultants to recruit personnel for vacancies supplied by the advertiser". Such invitations should be approached with great caution and checked out with solicitors, bank managers and the British Franchise Association.

What type of franchise are you getting?

Type of franchise:	Exclusive right to trade	Distributorship	Celebrity name Reg. trade mark	Pyramid selling	Business format franchising
Exclusive territory	√	√	X	☐	☐
Fee/royalty	√	☐	√	☐	√
Performance standards	√	√	☐	X	√
Agreement to hold stock	√	√	√	√	√
Training by franchisor	☐	☐	X	☐	√
Proven product method of operation	☐	X	X	X	√
Market survey by franchisor	☐	X	X	X	√
Back up by franchisor	☐	√	☐	X	√
Tied sources of supply	√	√	√	√	☐
Operating manual	☐	X	☐	√	√
Celebrity name/product	☐	☐	√	☐	X
Commission for recruiting others	☐	☐	X	√	X

√ = Yes
☐ = Sometimes
X = No

CHECKLIST 1

Is it a genuine business format franchise?

Use this checklist together with the chart on the previous page to make
sure that any franchise you examine meets the criteria for a business
format franchise. Remember, the further it departs from the business
format franchise formula, the greater the risks are likely to be and the
lower the potential value of what is on offer.

	Franchise option 1	Franchise option 2
1. Does the business being described as a franchise have all the ingredients of a genuine business format franchise? i.e.		
a) Features that are unique, either in terms of secret recipes or particular methods of operating		
b) That the form of business has been tested for a period of at least 18 months and found to work		
c) That you are being allotted an exclusive privileged territory and that a written report on its economic viability has been prepared and is available to you		
d) That adequate training and back-up services are provided initially and as required thereafter		
e) That the business is freely disposable at whatever point you choose, either on the open market or to the franchisor at a price which is assessed independently		
2. If you have to buy supplies from a particular source are you satisfied the franchisor has no undeclared interest in it?		
3. Are you satisfied that it is not a form of pyramid selling? (The signs of this would be that marketing the actual goods or services appears to be less important than recruiting new franchisees, and that your income is mainly going to be derived from the latter activity.)		
4. Is there a comprehensive manual to work from?		

13

	Franchise option 3	Franchise option 4
1. Does the business being described as a franchise have all the ingredients of a genuine business format franchise? i.e.		
a) Features that are unique, either in terms of secret recipes or particular methods of operating		
b) That the form of business has been tested for a period of at least 18 months and found to work		
c) That you are being allotted an exclusive privileged territory and that a written report on its economic viability has been prepared and is available to you		
d) That adequate training and back-up services are provided initially and as required thereafter		
e) That the business is freely disposable at whatever point you choose, either on the open market or to the franchisor at a price which is assessed independently		
2. If you have to buy supplies from a particular source are you satisfied the franchisor has no undeclared interest in it?		
3. Are you satisfied that it is not a form of pyramid selling? (The signs of this would be that marketing the actual goods or services appears to be less important than recruiting new franchisees, and that your income is mainly going to be derived from the latter activity.)		
4. Is there a comprehensive manual to work from?		

Franchise option 5	Franchise option 6	Franchise option 7	Franchise option 8

Case History 1

A printing franchise that leaves a good impression

Wren Hoskyns-Abrahall's family was in the printing business, but his own career took him first into the navy and then into retail management. A course at the London Business School gave him the idea that he would like to run his own show and it seemed a natural step to start a print shop: a combination of the two types of business he knew most about retailing and printing. He decided right away that the best way to go about it was by taking up a franchise. "Wren's Quickprint wouldn't have meant much in the marketplace and I couldn't afford to buy an established printing works. I decided to approach Prontaprint, whose 230 High Street print shops in the UK had a good reputation, to see if they had a suitable franchise available."

As it happened they had a franchisee who wanted to sell and whose business was close to where Wren was living. There was an exclusive territory: London SW18 (Prontaprint's London territories are related to postal codes). Its potential was obvious. "The huge Arndale Shopping Centre across the road is a hive of small businesses but the whole area is full of small firms of all kinds. Wandsworth is also a rapidly improving residential district – there are lots of professional people around who are customers for jobs like headed notepaper and visiting cards."

In fact the range of printing jobs handled by Prontaprint is enormous – it covers anything from business stationery to small booklets and from designing letterheads to folding and binding catalogues. Because printing is very much a business geared to local needs, Prontaprint gives franchisees an unusual amount of freedom to develop services in whatever direction is needed. For instance Wren Hoskyns-Abrahall's print shop is right next to Wandsworth Town Hall, so he has a dyeline copier which can copy documents up to A0 size – the very big dimensions that are used in planning applications. He has also now installed a computerised typesetting machine – one of the few Prontaprint franchisees to have one. But does he resent paying a 10% royalty, when he is doing so much on his own?

"Not at all," he says. "The back-up I get, plus the sheer value of the name makes it well worthwhile. I can ring up any time for advice on financial and tax matters. The technical support is good too. In this business you're constantly having to make quality decisions on purchases of anything from capital equipment to paper stocks and there's a lot of know-how available to help me choose the best buys. Prontaprint have recommended suppliers from whom we can buy very advantageously because of the collective buying power of the 230 outlets – but we're free to buy anywhere we like."

He also finds the back-up in terms of advertising good. Half the royalty is spent by Prontaprint on promotion and he is convinced that it gives real value for money – especially when it is co-ordinated with his own promotion by direct mail and leaflet drops to potential customers in the neighbourhood.

He has a formidable array of printing equipment on the premises – even a small printing press. So how much technical knowledge do you need to run an instant print franchise? "I'm perhaps lucky in knowing a bit about it but very few franchisees have a knowledge of printing – you pick up what you need as you go along and both the franchisor and the machine suppliers rally round if you get into deep water. There are four weeks of basic training, but the emphasis is on marketing and presentation rather than on the technical side. You can hire expertise – for instance I employ a typographic designer on my staff of four people – and Prontaprint will advise you on specialist staff selection. There are also regular free training courses on new technical developments as well as sales techniques."

You do, however, need money. Wren estimates that the start-up costs are around £30,000, of which £3,000 is the initial fee. However bank finance is not hard to get with an established franchise like Prontaprint.

The other essential is personal commitment. "I'm free – free to work 24 hours a day," he jokes. "One mustn't underestimate the enormous amount of time running your own business takes up – and the financial rewards are not great for the hours you put in. This is a successful business. It's going well, but in order to build it up, I'm ploughing back almost all my profits into equipment. On the other hand I'm building up a very saleable asset here – not that I want to sell."

The question of commitment is doubly important because instant printing is a very competitive business. True, Wren has the Prontaprint exclusive for SW18, but there are at least three other print shops in the vicinity. So how does he stay ahead of the competition?

"Well, I don't cut prices, for a start. We have a schedule suggested by the franchisor, but it's only a guideline. We compete on quality, reliability, speed and range – and of course all Prontaprint sites are highly visible. You can hardly go down a British High Street without seeing our name. That's one of the advantages of franchising. I run my own business – to a very large extent in my own way. But in its field, its name is as well known nationally as McDonalds or Marks and Spencer."

Section 2

Is franchising right for you?

This section will lead you through the questions you need to ask about yourself before embarking on a franchise business.

One of the business schools that runs courses for people who want to start a firm of their own begins the induction phase by asking them what they would "really" like to do. Some of them, of course, would genuinely rather run a small business than do anything else, but a surprising number confess to secret ambitions to be a farmer, a doctor, a writer, a deep sea fisherman, or whatever. The object of this exercise is to demonstrate the impracticability of many dreams: only a handful of writers make a living at it, it takes six years' intensive training to be a doctor and about as long to get the hang of farming or professional fishing. Similarly, while a great many people dream of self-employment, not everybody can turn the dream into reality – and not only for reasons of money. Indeed as we shall show in section 7, raising money is not nearly as difficult as it used to be.

Learning to be head cook and bottle washer

One big problem is that working on your own is utterly different from working for an organisation. There everything is compartmentalised and though you know your own neck of the woods – whether it be sales or marketing or financial management – pretty well, you generally know remarkably little about the others. "Someone" does the payroll, makes the buying decisions, produces the goods, prices them in a way that will make a profit and makes sure customers get to hear about them. "Someone" sees to it that the mail is opened in the morning, that the place is shut when the last person leaves and that the cleaners will come round in the evening to hoover the floors and empty the ashtrays.

As a self employed person, that "someone" is you. In other words you have to learn about a great many aspects of business that you never came into contact with before. Even if you are not directly concerned with them on a day to day basis, they are your responsibility.

Remember the tale of the Elves and the Shoemaker, where all the chores were done by the elves overnight? Some people turn to franchising as a form of self employment because they think that the franchisor will take on the role of the elves. That is not so.

As a franchisee, you have to do everything yourself

True, many franchisors will help you in the first weeks of operation by having someone from their headquarters keep an eye on things – in some cases even holding your hand full-time for a while. Quite a number thereafter maintain some kind of hot-line where you can get advice in emergencies and some can even put in expert/temporary staff if something goes dreadfully wrong or you fall ill. But as far as the day to day running of the business is concerned you are the head cook and bottle washer, except for whatever words of wisdom are contained in the operating manual.

If that document is properly put together by an experienced franchisor, it should free you in one important respect. All new ventures go through a learning curve, when you have to learn things by experience. In business that is usually an expensive process: your prices are too high or too low, the concept is not quite right, the staff to customer ratio is wrong

– the possibilities are endless. In franchising that has, or should have been all worked out by the franchisor and the operating manual gives you exact instructions on what you need to do to make things work. This leaves you free to concentrate on running the business. In this sense, "someone" is guiding you through the learning curve.

Some illusions you must lose

Nevertheless, it isn't an easy ride. Almost everyone who has started in self employment comments that it is incredibly hard work and that for quite a time the hourly rate, if you stop to think about it, is a bad joke. "It means freedom, certainly," a self-employed businessman said at a seminar recently. "Freedom to work fourteen hours a day, six days a week, for at least the first couple of years." Franchisors tend to hold out glowing prospects of high earnings within a few months. They seldom tell you how many hours you have to put in to achieve them. If you are under illusions that working for yourself means that you can knock off at 5.30, even when things are running smoothly, lose them quickly.

Can your family help?

You need the family on your side

It follows from all this that your family will not be seeing much of you for something like the next couple of years. One of the questions you have to ask yourself is how you – and they – view the prospect of your coming home at night only to get down to a couple of hours' more paperwork and maybe not being able to spare much more time off than Sunday afternoons. If you're a workaholic, they are probably used to it. If you are middle aged and your family life is not that close anyway it may not make much difference. But if you and your family have been used to regarding non-working hours as sacrosanct it can place a strain on relationships and that, in turn, can affect your working efficiency. For this reason it is advisable to put everyone in the picture of what might be involved in terms of time.

It may of course be that they are able and willing to help. There is, for instance, a tax advantage to getting your wife involved in the business because she can then claim the wife's earned income allowance of £2005 a year. To get this you will have to demonstrate to the tax inspector that she is actually doing something – typing invoices, helping with customers or dealing with telephone enquiries. But in any case it will be very useful to have someone undertake these services and the more members of your family are involved, the more they will be understanding about the pressure you are under. On the other hand, if you think working with your wife (or husband) would be a strain, then it would be far better to leave them right out of it, whatever short-term financial attractions there may be.

Leadership and discipline

Can you be tough with employees?

Employing members of your family raises the question of how tough you can bring yourself to be over matters like discipline. Franchisors impose quite strict standards of conduct, dress and behaviour on what goes on in the franchisee's business, because the feeling is that one badly run operation reflects badly on the others. That means you will have to keep a close watch on these things and be prepared to crack down on your nearest and dearest on occasion – and to make no distinction between them and any other employees you might have. Again, if you think that this would cause more problems than it would solve, the best course is to leave them out altogether. But whoever you employ you will have to be prepared to speak firmly to them, should the need arise.

Your own character

Are you too independent minded?

The ability to keep order and at the same time to run a happy ship quite often depends on how much confidence you have in yourself and how much pride you have in what you are doing. For this reason it is absolutely vital that the franchise should be in some area of business you actually enjoy, not just in something where you think you can make a couple of bob. So, if you don't think you would enjoy dealing with the public and their kids, you shouldn't be running a fast food operation – at least not without trying it for a couple of weeks first. Most franchisors will let you work for nothing in one of their franchises to give you some experience of what it is like. If the one that takes your interest does not, there are quite a number of franchises to choose from as we shall show in the next section, and new ones are constantly emerging.

Within your area of choice it is also very important that you know, like and trust the franchisor. Though franchisors tend to tell you that it is exactly the same as running your own business, this is not really so. There are a good many constraints on what you can and cannot do. This can cause a good deal of friction unless there is a basic personal respect and liking underpinning the relationship, but it also means that very independently minded people do not, in general, make good franchisees. If you hate being told what to do, maybe you should consider some other form of business. At any rate you should make sure that the degree of control exercised by the franchisor is acceptable to you.

Of course, hardly anyone is perfectly suited to any particular job. There will be aspects of it that you like better than others, or feel that you are better at. It is merely a question of deciding whether you and the job fit together sufficiently to make a go of it – or perhaps whether you need a partner who can complement the areas where you feel less confident. There is nothing to stop you taking up a franchise with a partner, though of course this has implications for the income you can expect to earn.

Checklist number 2 gives you some questions you should ask yourself in determining your course of action – be honest with your answers because the only person you will be fooling otherwise is yourself.

CHECKLIST 2

How well do you match the profile of the ideal franchisee? (Part 1)

The tests in this section are designed to help you to gain an insight into your aptitudes and how well they will serve you in running a franchise business. Be honest with yourself in completing them – after all, it's your future prosperity that's at stake.

1. DO YOU LIKE WORK?
   a) If the goal is something I want, I don't care how hard I work. ☑
   b) I don't believe in doing more than is necessary. ☐
   c) Putting something off until tomorrow isn't the end of the world. ☐
2. WHAT ABOUT SELF-MOTIVATION?
   a) I'm at my best when I'm working to a deadline. ☑
   b) I never need any kind of pressure to get going. ☐
   c) I hate being pressurised by anyone or anything. ☐
3. WHAT IS YOUR PERSEVERANCE FACTOR?
   a) I can stick at things so long as I'm interested in what I'm doing. ☐
   b) I'll finish the job, provided someone else hasn't screwed it up on the way. ☐
   c) I always see things through if I've undertaken to do them. ☑
4. CAN YOU TAKE ORDERS?
   a) No problem when the situation calls for it. ☑
   b) Yes, if I'm told why. ☐
   c) I don't like being told what to do. ☐
5. HOW ARE YOU AS A LEADER?
   a) I like to do things by consensus. ☑
   b) I have trouble in putting myself over as an effective person. ☐
   c) People usually follow me when and if I show them the way. ☑
6. ARE YOU A GOOD ORGANISER?
   a) I enjoy organising and things generally work out the way I've planned them. ☑
   b) I really prefer action to talk, but I'll do it if I have to. ☐
   c) I believe things generally turn out all right on the night. ☐
7. CAN YOU MAKE DECISIONS?
   a) I've always found that problems solve themselves in the end. ☐
   b) I think it's vital to make decisions, even if they're not always the right ones. ☑
   c) I take time to make up my mind and like to involve other people in the process. ☑

8. CAN YOU EXPECT HELP FROM YOUR FAMILY?
   a) My wife/husband has always wanted me to go on my own. ☐
   b) I don't believe in letting family considerations stand in the way of my career. ☐
   c) My family wouldn't be either a help or a hindrance. ☑

9. HOW DO YOU GET ON WITH CUSTOMERS?
   a) I haven't had much contact with them, but I believe I'm a fairly gregarious and extrovert person by nature. ☐
   b) I've always had an excellent relationship with them. ☑
   c) I'm a background boy/girl by temperament. ☐

10. HOW GOOD IS YOUR HEALTH?
    a) I'm a hundred per cent fit. ☐
    b) I have enough energy to do all the things I want to do. ☐
    c) I can still cope with most things, but I don't feel as fit as I used to do. ☐

The answers are given below. Give yourself three points for every first place you have scored, two for every second and one where your answer scores third place. 25-30 means that you have the right kind of qualities to start on your own. 15-25 indicates that you should probably try working in someone else's franchise or small business first, before taking the plunge. 15 or less means that you are probably not ready yet for franchising on your own!

1.abc 2.bac 3.cab 4.abc 5.cab 6.abc 7.bca 8.acb 9.bac 10.abc

Now ask your spouse, a close friend or someone else who knows you well to rate you on each of these questions. If their opinion of you differs from your own, you may need to think again.

CHECKLIST 3

How well do you match the profile of the ideal franchisee? (Part 2)

Listed below are 19 characteristics considered by banks and franchises as important in the selection of potential franchisees. Rate yourself against each of these characteristics on a 1-10 scale in the following way:

(A) by what you instinctively feel about yourself.

(B) by how your spouse or a close relative rates you.

(C) by how current or former working colleagues rate you.

Use the chart below to draw a graph of your scores. Then compare your profile with the ideal profile drawn from franchises and banks, shown overleaf.

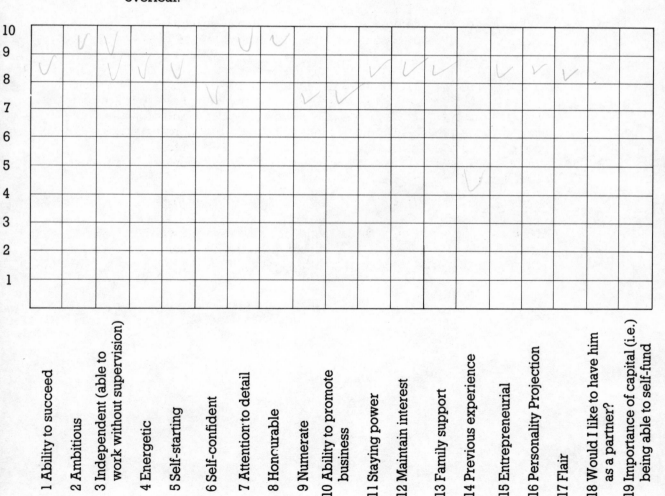

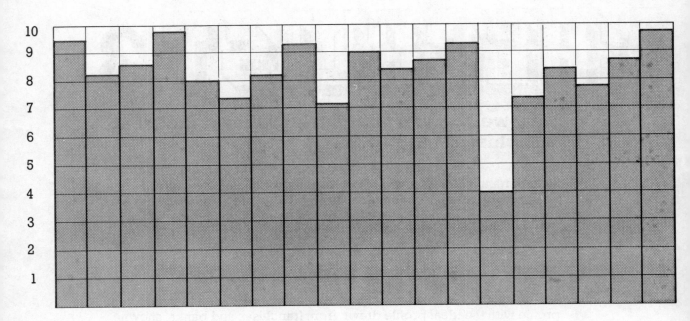

CHECKLIST 4

Are your plans fully prepared?

Use this checklist to make sure you are ready to set out on the road to your own business.

✔ **Yes**   ✔ **No**

1. Have you made an assessment of your skills, strengths and weaknesses and decided that operating a franchise is the right form of self-employment for you? Have you also tried to get a second opinion of that assessment?	☐ ☐
2. Have you made a list, as a result of the above, of the sort of franchises that you would like to go for?	☐ ☐
3. Have you made sure that these have a future, given present business and social trends?	☐ ☐
4. Do you plan to work with a partner? If so, have you worked with him or her before? If not, how do you know he or she would be the right person (i.e. do they have skills which complement yours?)	☐ ☐
5. Would you get help from members of your family? If you are planning to do so, have you assessed their skills and motivations in the same way as you have your own?	☐ ☐
6. If family help is not available, are you sure you can manage all aspects of the franchise on your own?	☐ ☐
7. If the answer to (6) is "no", does the franchisor's published financial calculations allow for the cost of hiring staff, if only on a temporary basis?	☐ ☐

Section 3

Choosing a franchise

What kind of franchise is best for you? This section examines the range of options available and provides guidelines on what to look for. Use checklist 5 to evaluate different franchises – but always seek professional advice before proceeding to a contract or parting with cash.

The range of business activities that are being franchised and their scope in terms of size and cost is already much wider than most people realise. Asked to name a franchise, the informed man in the street would probably mention Wimpy or Kentucky Fried Chicken. These are in fact two of the largest and longest established franchises in the UK in what is itself the biggest single sector in franchising: restaurants and fast foods. Even that sector, though, holds surprises. Not many people know that Holiday Inns are a franchise (though you would have to have substantial resources to be considered by them: an initial fee of £18,000 plus average start-up capital requirements of £35,000 a room; which probably accounts for the fact that there are only 5 UK Holiday Inn franchises in operation). Nor is it general knowledge that you have to have quite a lot of money to acquire a Wimpy Bar franchise – the start-up capital for one in a reasonably good location would now be over £170,000. Nonetheless there are well over 400 of them in the UK alone.

Start-up costs

How much
capital can you
put up?

Restaurants, in fact, are at the upper end of the investment range. Quite a number of them call for an input of £50,000 plus because of the high cost of acquiring and fitting out premises. Clearly, if you are hoping to attract passing trade a good location is essential – and good locations come expensive. This is also true of retail franchises, most of which require initial investments in the £15,000-£30,000 range. Those figures do not include the start-up fee charged by the franchisor.

Franchises which provide a service like cleaning, home beauty treatment, word processing or accounting – or indeed any activity that is supplied direct to a home or a business – are obviously less expensive, although continuing promotional costs to reach the market form a hidden extra, which the franchisor should draw to your attention. Even there, though, you will have to reckon with putting down £10,000 or more to start with. There is a growing sector below this level, however. Because a lot of people, particularly younger entrepreneurs and women have difficulty in raising these relatively large sums, there is now rapid growth in the so called "job franchises". These are in areas like home decorating or car repairs and often tend to be extensions of DIY activities into a money-earning role. Because they do not require premises, the capital outlay is usually relatively modest.

Types of franchise on offer

The choice of
franchise is
wide

Though you have to be realistic about relating investment to your resources and expectations of income from the franchise itself, there is very little inherent problem these days about raising money, provided you can make a good case to the bank – a subject which we will deal with in more detail in Section 7. It would be a great mistake to base your decision about what kind of franchising you choose to go into on what it costs rather on what you actually want to do and know you are good at. As we have indicated, the range of business format franchises is already quite wide and it is constantly growing. In the USA there are no less than 65 different kinds of franchises on offer, including many not yet seen here, such as in security services or employment agencies. However, there is a trend for business activities to spread from the USA to Europe, so if you see nothing suitable for you as yet, it may be worth looking at a list of US franchises quoted in such books as Martin Mendelsohn's *Guide to Franchising* (Pergamon Press). An example, for instance, of a US franchise concept that seems to be spreading over here is in professional services like accounting, where keeping a track of constantly changing legislation and tax rulings is getting beyond the capacity of many smaller firms.

Over the next ten years it is likely that the dozen or so types of franchises that have so far been identified by the British Franchising Association will be added to. At present the main UK categories are on:

Types of franchise
Beauty and health
Building and maintenance
Hotels and catering
Car maintenance and rental
Printing
Retailing
Cleaning

Information about franchises

One problem faced by people who want to get into franchising as a form of self-employment is keeping up with the details of franchises on offer. Some of these are advertised in the *Business to Business* sections of papers like *The Times* or *Sunday Times* but the fact that a franchise is being advertised even in a reputable paper is not necessarily proof that it is a good bet. Some franchisors, in fact, make a point of being very selective about who they take on and prefer people who have taken some trouble to seek them out, rather than appealing to all and sundry.

A regular update of new franchise opportunities is published in the quarterly magazine *Franchise World,* but it does not evaluate them, nor does it give the kind of information which will enable you or your advisers to do so. A good deal of guidance of this kind is however given in the book *Taking Up a Franchise* (Kogan Page). It contains information on such important details as ownership, fees and number of outlets on some sixty or so leading UK franchises, but, being a book, it naturally cannot keep up with all the new franchises that come on the market between editions. So what should you be looking for in making your initial enquiries if you cannot find out what you want from existing sources?

Checking on a franchise

Take a close look at the franchisor's track record

1. Franchising as an industry does not have a long history. The majority of business format franchises in the UK are less than five years old, so anything by way of a track record is often hard to establish. You should, however, try and find out how many UK franchise outlets are in operation and for how long they have been going. It is also important to know how many have been closed down or taken over by the franchisor – and for what reason.

The significance of exposure in the UK market is that several companies that have been successful in the USA have been less successful when they opened up here – what works in the USA does not necessarily transfer well to Europe. A case in point fairly recently was a big American ice cream franchisor. It caught a cold over here, because it turned out that people in Europe do not share the Americans' appetite for ice cream all the year round. So don't be too impressed by claims of a huge number of franchise outlets or big profits unless these have occurred in the UK.

Finding out how long they have been going is important because you want to be sure that the idea has been properly tested and the bugs have been taken out. You are, after all, paying your fee and royalty for a proven formula for success. Normally it takes about two years to establish that. If the franchisor makes the point that he is giving you the opportunity to come in on the ground floor, that should be reflected in a fairly modest scale of fees and royalties, because in effect you are sharing some of the risk.

Looking for steady growth

As for the number of franchises in operation, the ideal profile to look for is steady growth. Explosive expansion is not always good news for the franchisee, however profitable it may be for the franchisor. Under those circumstances, the franchisor may find himself overstretched when it comes to providing the back-up services that franchisees need. Another possibility to be aware of is that it could mean that the product or service is a craze, not built to last. (Remember skateboarding?)

Who owns the franchise?

2. It may be a moot point whether "who drives fat oxen should himself be fat" but unless the franchisor is making a success of the franchise, in terms of profitability and cash flow, it is unlikely that you will succeed where he has failed. The clue here will lie in the accounts filed at Companies House and your accountant should ask to see them, even if none have yet been filed. In fact if no accounts have been filed in the last two years be very careful. At worst they have something to hide (almost certainly so, if a sight of the accounts is refused) at best they are sloppy in their methods and you will be at the receiving end of that once you start working with them.

How committed is the franchisor?

From a safety point of view the best franchise to be in with is one that is owned by a substantial company. For instance, Wimpy is owned by United Biscuits. Another plus point is heavy financial involvement by the franchisor is in the enterprise, as indicated by amount of *issued* share capital. (*Authorised* share capital is fairly meaningless in this context.) Not to get too technical about it, the issued share capital in a limited company represents the amount of the shareholders' financial liability if things go wrong. You can form a limited company with an issued share capital of as little as £2. If a company has a low capital base compared to the extent of its activities, this may imply a reluctance by the owners to put their money where their mouth is.

Another check, of course, is whether they are members of the British Franchise Association. Though this is essentially a body for franchisors, the code of conduct it requires them to observe also extends a certain amount of protection to franchisees as does the fact that a condition of membership is that the franchisor has to have been in business for three years and to have operated at least three franchises successfully. But that code has no legal force, nor are the BFA infallible. One of their recent members was a company that went bankrupt in thoroughly disgraceful circumstances that were disclosed on the BBC's "Checkpoint" programme. That programme also drew attention to the plight of franchisees when the franchisor goes out of business, whatever the circumstances. It pays to hitch your wagon to a star.

Beware of cowboys – check the franchisor's background carefully

3. The business world has its share of crooks, cowboys and con-men. Franchising, where the naive, inexperienced or careless can sometimes be persuaded to part with quite large sums of money for what can be a pretty vague business concept or "format" sadly attracts some of them. The same names keep on cropping up in this context, though the companies through which they operate change their name as they disappear with the loot. The practice is known as "change the name and do the same". British company law is regrettably lax in controlling such activities, as investigative financial journalists frequently point out. When the franchise is new, when the BFA knows nothing about it, when the issued share capital is small and where you are asked for a high initial fee even when – indeed especially when – the royalty is low, your accountant should check very carefully into the antecedents and previous activities of the owners of the franchise.

This is particularly important because franchisees do not enjoy a great deal of legal protection from franchisors who, for instance, take their money and do very little in return for it; and once you have signed a contract, however inequitable or irksome you find it to be in practice, there is very little you can do to get out of it. Sharp practitioners, you will find, also have the knack of employing sharp solicitors.

Does the franchisor have the resources he needs to give the support promised?

4. You also have to beware of the inexperienced franchisor – anybody can start a franchise and because it is a good way of expanding a business without investment, some entrepreneurs have tried to become franchisors without the resources to do so. In the next chapter we will look in more detail at what you ought to expect in the way of back-up, but at the preliminary stage it is important to know whether the franchisor has the wherewithal to give you the kind of training and staff back-up facilities that he should. One simple but effective test is to look at his offices. Their physical appearance can be most revealing, though an improbable display of affluence in relation to the scope and nature of the operation could be just as much an occasion for caution as the sight of a small scruffy room with unemptied ashtrays and decrepit office furniture. Another good test is, of course, to look at other franchises he operates and, even more, to talk to the people running them.

Is the franchisor as choosey as you are?

5. The franchisor should be as discriminating about his franchisees as you are about him. He should ask you about your motivation, experience and resources as searchingly as you have put such questions to yourself in the previous chapter.

CHECKLIST 5

Checking out the franchisor

Use this checklist to compare the franchises you are considering. Make sure you get all the answers.

	Franchise option 1	Franchise option 2
1. How long has the franchise been operating in the UK?		
2. How many outlets have been established in that time?		
3. How many have been closed down or bought back by the franchisor and for what reasons?		
4. If it is a new or a recent franchise, how long has the franchisor run his pilot operation, and has it been tried out in areas comparable to the one you are being offered?		
5. Is the franchise a subsidiary or otherwise part of another organisation. If so, who are they and what are their other activities? Will those affect you in any way (e.g. having to get your supplies from them)?		
6. Who are the franchisor company's directors and what is their business background? Have they ever been involved with a venture that failed?		
7. Have they filed an up to date set of accounts at Companies House?		
8. What is their issued share capital?		

	Franchise option 1	Franchise option 2
9. What is the size and composition of their headquarters staff?		
10. Are they members of the British Franchise Association?		
11. Will you be allowed to talk freely to any of their existing franchisees – selected by you?		
12. Are you being allowed to make your decisions freely and without direct or indirect pressure to make up your mind quickly?		
13. Have you sought an independent view from a solicitor, accountant or bank manager regarding the franchisor's status and claims?		
14. Have you satisfied yourself at first hand that the product or service is competitive with others on the market and that there will be a continuing demand for it in the proposed franchise territory?		
15. Has the franchisor taken steps to find out about you and your resources, background and experience – or has he given you the impression that he would take on anyone with the price of an initial fee about them?		

	Franchise option 3	Franchise option 4
1. How long has the franchise been operating in the UK?		
2. How many outlets have been established in that time?		
3. How many have been closed down or bought back by the franchisor and for what reasons?		
4. If it is a new or a recent franchise, how long has the franchisor run his pilot operation, and has it been tried out in areas comparable to the one you are being offered?		
5. Is the franchise a subsidiary or otherwise part of another organisation. If so, who are they and what are their other activities? Will those affect you in any way (e.g. having to get your supplies from them)?		
6. Who are the franchisor company's directors and what is their business background? Have they ever been involved with a venture that failed?		
7. Have they filed an up to date set of accounts at Companies House?		
8. What is their issued share capital?		

	Franchise option 3	Franchise option 4
9. What is the size and composition of their headquarters staff?		
10. Are they members of the British Franchise Association?		
11. Will you be allowed to talk freely to any of their existing franchisees – selected by you?		
12. Are you being allowed to make your decisions freely and without direct or indirect pressure to make up your mind quickly?		
13. Have you sought an independent view from a solicitor, accountant or bank manager regarding the franchisor's status and claims?		
14. Have you satisfied yourself at first hand that the product or service is competitive with others on the market and that there will be a continuing demand for it in the proposed franchise territory?		
15. Has the franchisor taken steps to find out about you and your resources, background and experience – or has he given you the impression that he would take on anyone with the price of an initial fee about them?		

	Franchise option 5	Franchise option 6
1. How long has the franchise been operating in the UK?		
2. How many outlets have been established in that time?		
3. How many have been closed down or bought back by the franchisor and for what reasons?		
4. If it is a new or a recent franchise, how long has the franchisor run his pilot operation, and has it been tried out in areas comparable to the one you are being offered?		
5. Is the franchise a subsidiary or otherwise part of another organisation. If so, who are they and what are their other activities? Will those affect you in any way (e.g. having to get your supplies from them)?		
6. Who are the franchisor company's directors and what is their business background? Have they ever been involved with a venture that failed?		
7. Have they filed an up to date set of accounts at Companies House?		
8. What is their issued share capital?		

	Franchise option 5	Franchise option 6
9. What is the size and composition of their headquarters staff?		
10. Are they members of the British Franchise Association?		
11. Will you be allowed to talk freely to any of their existing franchisees – selected by you?		
12. Are you being allowed to make your decisions freely and without direct or indirect pressure to make up your mind quickly?		
13. Have you sought an independent view from a solicitor, accountant or bank manager regarding the franchisor's status and claims?		
14. Have you satisfied yourself at first hand that the product or service is competitive with others on the market and that there will be a continuing demand for it in the proposed franchise territory?		
15. Has the franchisor taken steps to find out about you and your resources, background and experience – or has he given you the impression that he would take on anyone with the price of an initial fee about them?		

	Franchise option 7	Franchise option 8
1. How long has the franchise been operating in the UK?		
2. How many outlets have been established in that time?		
3. How many have been closed down or bought back by the franchisor and for what reasons?		
4. If it is a new or a recent franchise, how long has the franchisor run his pilot operation, and has it been tried out in areas comparable to the one you are being offered?		
5. Is the franchise a subsidiary or otherwise part of another organisation. If so, who are they and what are their other activities? Will those affect you in any way (e.g. having to get your supplies from them)?		
6. Who are the franchisor company's directors and what is their business background? Have they ever been involved with a venture that failed?		
7. Have they filed an up to date set of accounts at Companies House?		
8. What is their issued share capital?		

	Franchise option 7	Franchise option 8
9. What is the size and composition of their headquarters staff?		
10. Are they members of the British Franchise Association?		
11. Will you be allowed to talk freely to any of their existing franchisees – selected by you?		
12. Are you being allowed to make your decisions freely and without direct or indirect pressure to make up your mind quickly?		
13. Have you sought an independent view from a solicitor, accountant or bank manager regarding the franchisor's status and claims?		
14. Have you satisfied yourself at first hand that the product or service is competitive with others on the market and that there will be a continuing demand for it in the proposed franchise territory?		
15. Has the franchisor taken steps to find out about you and your resources, background and experience – or has he given you the impression that he would take on anyone with the price of an initial fee about them?		

Case History 2

A cautionary tale

In November 1982, Ziebart GB Ltd, a vehicle rust proofing franchise, went into liquidation. It was so well-known as to form a case study in one of the standard books on franchising, Mendelsohn's *Guide to Franchising*, where it is described in fairly glowing terms. It had the unusual feature that franchisees did not pay a royalty – just an initial fee of £5100. The company presumably made its further income from providing the sealant that was the unique formula for its success and the first result was that franchisees could no longer get the sealant – but that, as it turned out, was the least of their problems. According to the BBC programme "Checkpoint", the sealant was far from effective, though one of its sales points was that franchisees gave their customers an unlimited 10 year guarantee against failure. Franchisees *thought* that when they bought the sealant from Ziebart they also bought insurance against claims and so they did – for one year only. After that, they were on their own, a vital piece of information that was concealed in the small print. Consequently several of them are now facing hefty claims for failure of the process.

Ziebart franchisees were left high and dry, but some have reported that they were subsequently approached by a company with a very similar name and offering a very similar service asking them to put down a sum of money for a rust-proofing franchise! Presumably none did, but it shows that there are no limits to brass neck; presumably also, some entrepreneurs new to the field are putting their hard earned savings into what they think is a nice little business.

Moral 1. Read the fine print carefully – ignorance is no defence when it comes to an argument about the contract.
Moral 2. Find out if the process has been tested for long enough for the snags, if any, to show.

Section 4

What you should get for your money

This section outlines the basics that you should expect the franchisor to provide. It also shows you the questions to ask existing holders of a franchise. Checklist 6 will help you evaluate whether what is offered is worth the money.

The exact nature of the agreement between yourself and the franchisor is spelled out in the contract, but before you start going through that document and thinking about its implications you should consider what you have a right to expect from it in broad terms. The franchisor will be taking an initial fee which, as we have seen, usually runs into several thousand pounds, plus a continuing percentage of your takings. What do you get for your money and how good a bargain is it likely to be?

● In the first place you get a product or service which naturally will be described to you in glowing terms. But quite apart from the element of salesmanship, there is a natural tendency on the part of anyone who has got hold of a good idea or product to think it is the hottest thing since sliced bread – irrespective of the fact that there may be others around that are very similar. The questions you have to ask are

Will the business last?

1. What are the competing products or services?

2. How do they compare in price?

3. If the product or service is unique, how does the franchisor plan to keep it that way?

4. Does it have staying power?

5. Is it a growth market – or merely one that has grown rapidly in the past?

There is no need to be afraid of a new idea, provided the franchisors take a realistic view of the future. For instance, Chromacopy, a colour copying service that has seen a very fast growth rate, is well aware of the likelihood of competitors coming into a market it has largely to itself at the moment, but it is concentrating its efforts on establishing a reputation for speed as well as quality – not just relying on the concept alone.

Do you get an "exclusive territory" or similar guarantee?

● Most franchises carry with them the guarantee of an "exclusive territory" – the contract often shows this on a map. That's fine, but remember that there may be other franchises in it, offering a similar product – not to mention non-franchise competitors. Furthermore there is nothing to stop "your" customers crossing the border and going to franchisees in the adjoining territory. In point of fact exclusive territories are illegal under EEC trade regulations, though in practice these tend to be applied more to larger companies. However, one of the newest franchises, Regional Business Services, does not grant exclusive territories for this reason, but instead – undertakes to keep outlets a reasonable distance apart. That may become more widespread.

● In Australia there are farms as big as English counties – very impressive until you find out that the land is so barren that it only supports three sheep to an acre. Beware of the "three-sheep syndrome". It is possible to have franchise territories that look very extensive on paper but that are of limited commercial value because:

| Do you have sufficient market data on customers and competition? | – There are too many well established competitors close by, e.g. two fast print shops serving one neighbourhood. |
| | |

Do you have sufficient market data on customers and competition?

– There are too many well established competitors close by, e.g. two fast print shops serving one neighbourhood.

– The social and economic mix is wrong, e.g. a fast food operation in a business area that is dead at night.

– There are physical problems of access, e.g. a retail outlet with double yellow lines on the pavement outside.

The market survey of the territory referred to in section 1 should have covered these points and should tell you about the number, spending power and consumer habits of your potential customers, as well as about your competitors. The site itself should also have been checked for planning permission and the impact of possible future local authority plans on it.

Is any rent reasonable?

● Related to the economic value of site and territory is the question of rent, when the franchisor owns the freehold. Is the rent reasonable by local standards for businesses with similar expectations of turnover and profit? The best way to find out is to go round and ask – never take any claims by the franchisor for granted. He will not respect you less for doing your homework because you have a mutual interest in the success of the venture. If his attitude is otherwise, be very much on your guard.

How substantial is the training you receive?

● All franchises will involve training. The question here is whether it is sufficiently well organised and systematic to set you on the road to success. The comments and criticisms of other franchisees – and you should certainly make a point of talking to them – will be useful here. Another good pointer is the operating manual. If this is well organised and well-written it is probable that the franchisor's training is in good hands; if it is scruffy and out of date, it is equally probable that it will not be.

It is also relevant to ask, in these days of increasingly complex legislation, whether training will be provided in such matters as handling VAT returns or complying with employment law requirements – or whether it applies to the operational side only.

How much of the advertising will be local?

● Advertising and publicity is an important part of the franchise package and the franchisor often commits himself to spending part of the royalty you pay him on promoting the franchise. The question there is how much of that money will be devoted to advertising your particular outlet in local media. You will, of course, gain something from national advertising for the franchise as a whole, but you will undoubtedly have to create some local awareness as well. Who will pay for that?

Is the price of supplies reasonable?

● One of the advantages attributed to franchising is that it gives franchisees some of the economic muscle of a large organisation while still retaining a large amount of "small is beautiful" type independence – for instance in bulk purchasing supplies. However, the franchisor may use that muscle for his own purposes and not pass on any discounts. He may even load prices as a means of getting extra revenue, so it is important to know whether you are getting value for money in this respect. Certainly there should be some option to getting supplies from a source nominated by the franchisor and in fact EEC trade laws may shortly prohibit monopoly arrangements.

This, however, begins to take us into the real nature of the relationship between franchisor and franchisee and that is governed by the contract which we will discuss in Section 6.

What should you be looking for, though, if you are buying an existing franchise, rather than dealing with the franchisor in a green field situation?

Buying an existing outlet

Buying a going concern may be less risky

Many of the points you need to consider are in fact exactly the same; that is, you need to evaluate the product, the territory and the credibility of the franchisor – and hence of his income and profit forecast. But you have one big advantage. Instead of being dependent on prophecies based on what has happened elsewhere, you will have some real history to go on.

The first question to ask is obviously why the existing franchisee is selling and to satisfy yourself that the reason is a good one. The fact that he (or she – an increasing number of franchisees these days are women) cannot make a living at it may not be the fault of the franchise – the franchisee may not be suited to self-employment – but it is doubly difficult to succeed where others have failed because usually the business has gone downhill in the process. Few sellers will admit to that kind of reason, though – they will usually say that they are moving to another area, or have decided to become completely independent; whatever, in fact, sounds convincing.

The clue to the truth will almost certainly be in the accounts and you should really get a sharp and experienced accountant to look at them – not just a bookkeeper, glorified or otherwise. One reason is that the owners of most businesses distort the financial picture just a bit. If the picture is not too rosy they will try to convince you that it is much better than it has been made to look, in order to minimise tax. Equally if it appears to be highly profitable, check whether that profit includes a fair figure for the owner's drawings – and whether you might need to increase certain costs; for instance, take on staff in order to make a go of things.

Buying an existing franchise from a franchisee often gives more scope for bargaining than dealing direct with a franchisor, who would not normally deviate much from the initial fee, though he may be prepared to accept staged payment. One reason is that whereas the franchisor can afford to wait, a person selling an existing business does not usually want to hang around too long. One thing a purchaser needs to check, though, is whether the vendor has cleared his right to sell with the franchisor. Normally he would have to give him first refusal or to have the purchaser vetted by the franchisor – often both. The ultimate golden rule, though (and it applies to a new franchise as much as to an existing one) is never be rushed into making a decision on the grounds that there are other buyers waiting to snap up this fantastic bargain. It is the oldest sales trick in the world, and you should beware of any seller who tries it on.

Some leading questions you must ask

Before spending time – and usually money – on investigating a franchise offer, whether from an existing franchisee who wants to sell, or a franchisor, you should talk to other franchisees of the same business format. Choose one who hasn't got an axe to grind (because he wants to sell you his business or who has been picked out by the franchisor).

Talk to existing holders of the franchise

The leading questions are:

1. How long have you operated the franchise?

2. How accurate have the franchisor's forecasts of sales, costs and profits turned out to be?

3. Have the rewards been commensurate with the amount of work put in?

4. How helpful has the franchisor been in terms of marketing and administrative back-up?

5. Was the training adequate?

6. Does the operating manual cover most of the eventualities and is it easy to follow?

7. Are there any clauses in the contract that you wish you had tried to get altered?

8. Would you choose this form of business again, knowing what you now know about it?

CHECKLIST 6

Sizing up value for money

Is the franchise worth the money? Use the answers to these questions to put a cash value on the business.

	Franchise option 1	Franchise option 2
A. 1. What special features does the franchise have to make it different from competing services and products?		
2. Is it in a market that is still growing and likely to last?		
3. Has the franchisor produced a written market survey of the proposed territory?		
4. Do you have exclusive rights or some other similar form of protection?		
5. Are rents in line with those of the neighbourhood?		
6. What initial and ongoing training will be provided?		
7. How much of your royalty will be devoted to advertising? How much of that will be local to your operation?		

	Franchise option 1	Franchise option 2
8. To what extent will you be free to buy products other than from the franchisor?		
B. 1. If you are buying an existing franchise, is there a good reason for the owner to sell?		
2. Have you had the books examined by an accountant to make sure the figures tally with the reasons given for the sale?		
3. Have you seen the lease, been satisfied with its provisions and had the property surveyed if this has not been recently done?		
4. Have you talked frankly to other franchisees?		

	Franchise option 3	Franchise option 4
A. 1. What special features does the franchise have to make it different from competing services and products?		
2. Is it in a market that is still growing and likely to last?		
3. Has the franchisor produced a written market survey of the proposed territory?		
4. Do you have exclusive rights or some other similar form of protection?		
5. Are rents in line with those of the neighbourhood?		
6. What initial and ongoing training will be provided?		
7. How much of your royalty will be devoted to advertising? How much of that will be local to your operation?		

	Franchise option 3	Franchise option 4
8. To what extent will you be free to buy products other than from the franchisor?		
B. 1. If you are buying an existing franchise, is there a good reason for the owner to sell?		
2. Have you had the books examined by an accountant to make sure the figures tally with the reasons given for the sale?		
3. Have you seen the lease, been satisfied with its provisions and had the property surveyed if this has not been recently done?		
4. Have you talked frankly to other franchisees?		

	Franchise option 5	Franchise option 6
A. 1. What special features does the franchise have to make it different from competing services and products?		
2. Is it in a market that is still growing and likely to last?		
3. Has the franchisor produced a written market survey of the proposed territory?		
4. Do you have exclusive rights or some other similar form of protection?		
5. Are rents in line with those of the neighbourhood?		
6. What initial and ongoing training will be provided?		
7. How much of your royalty will be devoted to advertising? How much of that will be local to your operation?		

	Franchise option 5	Franchise option 6
8. To what extent will you be free to buy products other than from the franchisor?		
B. 1. If you are buying an existing franchise, is there a good reason for the owner to sell?		
2. Have you had the books examined by an accountant to make sure the figures tally with the reasons given for the sale?		
3. Have you seen the lease, been satisfied with its provisions and had the property surveyed if this has not been recently done?		
4. Have you talked frankly to other franchisees?		

	Franchise option 7	Franchise option 8
A. 1. What special features does the franchise have to make it different from competing services and products?		
2. Is it in a market that is still growing and likely to last?		
3. Has the franchisor produced a written market survey of the proposed territory?		
4. Do you have exclusive rights or some other similar form of protection?		
5. Are rents in line with those of the neighbourhood?		
6. What initial and ongoing training will be provided?		
7. How much of your royalty will be devoted to advertising? How much of that will be local to your operation?		

	Franchise option 7	Franchise option 8
8. To what extent will you be free to buy products other than from the franchisor?		
B. 1. If you are buying an existing franchise, is there a good reason for the owner to sell?		
2. Have you had the books examined by an accountant to make sure the figures tally with the reasons given for the sale?		
3. Have you seen the lease, been satisfied with its provisions and had the property surveyed if this has not been recently done?		
4. Have you talked frankly to other franchisees?		

A fast food franchise that left a bad taste*

When Jim Ellis was made redundant from his job as a manager in the shipping department of a Midlands manufacturing firm, he received quite a generous golden handshake – 18 months' salary. After six unsuccessful months of trying to find another job he got in touch with a careers consultant, who told him that at his age – 48 – he might find re-employment difficult. Had he considered starting up a business of his own? Jim said that he didn't feel that he had enough experience to do that, but the consultant said he knew someone who might be able to help him. "To tell the truth, I wasn't terribly impressed with the chap," Jim remembers. "But sure enough, a few days later I got a brochure through the post, headed "A CHANCE TO BREAK OUT OF THE UNEMPLOYMENT TRAP".

It had obviously been sent at the suggestion of the consultant to whom he had spoken and set out what appeared to be an excellent idea for starting your own business. "It was described as a franchise," Jim says. "The brochure outlined what that was. It explained it was in some ways like the local radio franchises out of which franchisees had made millions, only it was even better because you got a tried and tested

*For legal reasons this case study is a composite of the experiences of several franchisees dealing with different franchisors. All characters and companies mentioned are fictitious.

business idea, training and general operating back-up. This particular one was in fast food, which they described as the most rapidly growing service business in the country. But they pointed out that the risks of going it alone were very high, whereas in franchising, because everything was piloted first, you had a 90% chance of success. To take on a business concept that had been fully tested, there was, of course, a start-up fee that reflected the enormous development costs – in the USA, which the brochure said was the world's most competitive and sophisticated market. The initial fee was £4000, but the total start-up costs came to £7000 – the rest was for equipment, a van, initial supplies, stationery and so forth."

The particular fast food concept involved was providing a bring-in sandwich service called SANDWICH AIRLIFT, designed for offices and businesses. The brochure pointed out how bad most take-away sandwiches were, how people had to queue up for them, how expensive full-scale lunches were and how bad for your waistline. With the Sandwich Airlift concept on the other hand, you simply telephoned your order from a list of very tasty-sounding fillings, which were prepared by the franchisee from "secret recipes" which the franchisee would be shown how to prepare in an operating manual. "Some of them sounded a bit American for our market," Jim says. "But the idea as a whole seemed like a good one. If you have an hour for lunch, you don't want to spend ten minutes queuing in a sandwich bar, and if you're in a hurry sandwiches at your desk could be a real boon."

He sent off for further particulars and shortly thereafter he had a call from the "London Vice-President" of the firm. No, there was no need for him to come down to London. Mr Zwicker would be very happy to meet him in Birmingham for lunch and a very good lunch it was. "He told me that I was getting in on the ground floor of something really good. They had 400 franchises operating in the USA and Canada where some franchisees were making profits in the order of $30,000–$40,000 a year. Because they'd only recently launched it in the UK, the franchises were still cheap. He told me that he'd be very surprised if it wouldn't be worth ten times what I'd paid for it in five years time – that a franchise was just like running your own business, only better, because you got the benefit of the franchisor's business know-how. In fact they felt so confident about it that they'd buy the business back from me any time I wanted to get out."

Zwicker explained to Jim Ellis that he would get an exclusive territory. "He had it drawn up on a map and sure enough it included a lot of very good prospects: medium-sized offices of the sort of firms that have money, even in a recession, like lawyers and accountants. There were also a couple of biggish insurance firms and finance houses. Zwicker said they'd done a survey of the area and they reckoned I could easily make a profit of £12,000 a year from it. With the tax advantage of running my own business he told me I'd get my money back in about 18 months." Another attractive feature was the royalty. It was only 5% and Zwicker said that was a lot less than the going rate for fast food of about 8%. They were able to keep it low because – and he said he'd be frank about this – they made money on supplying ingredients to franchisees. You had to buy from them, but he said their bulk buying power made them very competitive. No, he was sorry but you could only sell sandwiches with the franchisor's "own brand" filling. "That's what makes us distinctive – otherwise we'd be just another sandwich place," he explained. The actual recipes for putting them together were contained in an operating manual which covered most situations you were likely to meet. There was also a training course: quite a short one, because it was really a very simple method. No, it wasn't at their head office. They ran it at a hotel in the north-east.

"I said that it all sounded pretty good," Jim remembers. "And that I'd like to show the proposal to my bank manager. Zwicker was very pleasant about it, but he said that was bound to delay things and that he had another chap in the area who was dead keen and ready to sign up – in fact he was going on to see him after lunch. He said he was under a lot of pressure from his head office to tie up the franchise within the next few days. Frankly, he said, that I was the kind of highly motivated guy who'd make a success of that kind of business, but that he really needed a decision by the end of the following week. However, he said that he did see that raising £7000 wasn't going to be easy for me. A couple of days later he phoned to say that he'd discussed the matter with New York and he said that the company themselves would make me a loan of £2000 at commercial rates. So I signed up."

The training courses seemed a bit perfunctory. There were half a dozen franchisees on it and they were shown how to make the sandwich fillings and given a course on marketing. It was based on an American text and all the terminology was American. "It didn't seem relevant to the UK at all," Jim Ellis said. "It was all high pressure salesmanship and wouldn't have worked here. I used my own methods to call on the businesses in my area to try to get them to take my bring-in service."

That was when the first snags struck him. Trade was not nearly as easy to get as Zwicker had said and the American ingredients and descriptions were treated with a good deal of caution. People thought it was a great idea, but what they wanted was beef, cheese and tomato, smoked salmon and so forth; not "Polish fresh baked rye, overstuffed with Mother Kowalski's home-made ham sausage", to give one example. The other big problem was that the business really took two people to run. You needed one person to make the sandwiches and the deliveries and another to get the customers, take telephone messages and so forth. The £12,000 projection offered by Zwicker was a reasonable starting income for one person, but looked a lot less healthy divided between two, even if the other person was Jim's wife.

Jim discussed the problem of ingredients and descriptions with Zwicker, who was very reasonable about it. "Sure, we'll change whatever doesn't work," he said. "That's why the start-up costs are low – we're still experimenting. We'll change the names around – call it a Henry VIII sandwich. How about that?"

Such modifications made a slight difference, but there was another difficulty that Zwicker had not explained and that Jim now wished he'd pressed him about. Deliveries of ingredients only happened once a week and, in fact, were often late. Jim found he had to buy a deep freeze to accommodate the stock he needed and that had not been allowed for in Sandwich Airlift's cost projections. Also, it was very difficult to estimate just what kind of ingredients would be in demand and he and his wife had to eat a lot of their own products. Furthermore, the ingredients were by no means cheap and what with the cost of the deep freeze, food wastage and unexpectedly high marketing and delivery costs, it was clear after six months that the £12,000 profit target had been wildly optimistic. He tried to discuss these problems with Zwicker, but he found that the phone was either engaged or that Zwicker was "in conference and would call him back". He never did.

"I realised that I'd made a terrible mistake," Jim tells. "Then I remembered that Zwicker had promised to buy the business back any time, if it didn't work. I went to see him and when I did so I got quite a shock. All I could see of Sandwich Airlift was a scruffy one-room office. Zwicker said he didn't remember saying anything about a buy-back arrangement. Where in the contract was there any such clause? Furthermore, he said I was falling behind on my repayments of the £2000 loan and threatened me with legal action."

A few weeks later Jim got a letter from a London solicitor saying that Sandwich Airlift had ceased trading, but that he was still due to repay their loan. His own solicitor has suggested that he should ignore the demand and has threatened a counter-suit under the Trade Descriptions Act. Jim is now running an ordinary take-away and bring-in sandwich business and has hopes of making a go of it – but he has lost his entire investment in the now-defunct franchise. So where did he go wrong?

"Obviously I shouldn't have signed the contract without making sure that Zwicker's promises were there in black and white, and without talking to the bank and to my solicitor," he says. "They would have pointed out that the initial fee was suspiciously high – I'm told it shouldn't be more than 20% of the start-up costs at the absolute outside. I should have been alerted by the fact that Zwicker wasn't keen for me to talk to them. I should also have talked to other franchisees – they would have experienced the same problems as I found. And I should have checked Zwicker out with the British Franchise Association. My solicitor found that he'd been involved with several dubious franchise ventures previously."

Section 5

Professional advisers and how to choose them

This section discusses how to get the best out of professional advisers, and how to discover when they are not necessarily representing your best interests.

Professional services are expensive and so is professional advice. There are, it is true, various forms of free advice, but it has often been said that "there is no such thing as a free lunch"; either there is some indirect and hidden charge or the adviser has some interest in the advice he gives you. The latter case is not necessarily harmful: your bank manager has an interest in seeing you set up on a sound footing, because that way he ensures that the money he lends you is safe; an insurance broker has an interest in seeing that you are properly covered because that is how he earns his commission; the Government's Small Firms Service will advise you because that is their job and it is paid for by the taxpayer. But in general, if someone offers you free professional advice, ask yourself where the catch is.

Franchise advisers

Check out "franchise consultants" carefully

This is a point to bear in mind over the services offered by franchise advisers or consultants. The Small Firms Service points out that:

"There are a number of people or organisations who describe themselves as 'franchise consultants'. But it should be remembered that there are no legal restrictions on the use of such a description and that there are no formal qualifications to be obtained before opening business as a franchise consultant."

Will the consultant let you talk to his other clients?

If they are not charging you for their services, someone else must be paying: you've guessed it – the franchisor. In fact advisers have even been known to wear two hats, the other being that they are themselves owners of the franchise they are recommending. It is more common, of course, for the more questionable "franchise advisers" to be receiving a commission from franchisors, and the quality of franchisors who resort to such methods must be a matter of concern. In the absence of legislation, it is ultimately up to you to create your own safeguards in such a situation. The most effective one would be to ask the franchise adviser to confirm, in writing, that he has no undisclosed financial interest in any franchise he recommends. You should also ask him how many successful franchises he has advised and whether you can pick out two or three of those at random to talk to. These questions should be put irrespective of whether or not you are paying a fee for advice – that, in itself, is not a guarantee of its impartiality. If a fee is involved, establish beforehand exactly what it is and what you will get for your money.

The small firms service

DoI Small Firms Centres will give independent advice

The Department of Industry has set up some 16 Small Firms Centres throughout the country. They have no special expertise in franchising, though their staff will provide a certain amount of free advice on the sort of questions you ought to ask about the franchisor and about the franchise generally. They also have a number of free and useful booklets on various aspects of running a small business.

Local conditions tend to have a considerable bearing on the chances for a small business to succeed. In recognition of this fact many local authorities have set up enterprise agencies, often staffed by experienced managers seconded from industries in the neighbourhood who can advise you on such matters as competition or new opportunities opening up in the area. Ask the Small Firms Service for the name of the nearest one. Alternatively there is a list of them in a useful book published by the BBC: *The Small Business Guide* by Colin Barrow. Their advice has been found to be very useful by a number of new entrepreneurs.

Your bank manager

The banks –
some now
have franchise
specialists

Bank managers are more aware of franchising than they used to be and two of the clearing banks, Barclays and Natwest, have set up central franchising units to advise their branch managers. Williams & Glynn's have also now appointed a senior manager with special responsibility in this sphere.

The people in charge of these units are extremely knowledgeable about the range of franchises on offer and through the banks' formidable intelligence network also have a considerable inside information on individual franchisors as well as trends and prospects within the industry. You can approach them either direct or through your local branch, who will refer specific queries to their head office.

As with most forms of professional advice, you have to be clear about what an enquiry can deliver. The central franchise unit of a big bank cannot tell you what sort of franchise you should take up, for instance – but if you come along with a specific proposal they can give you an impartial opinion on whether the franchisor's financial forecast looks realistic and to what extent the bank can help you raise the money that will be needed. They may even be eloquently silent or non-committal about the franchisor – in which case, take the hint; do not pass "GO", as they say in Monopoly.

If you have approached the franchising unit at head office direct, they will pass your name on to your nearest good and suitable bank manager – the banks acknowledge that not all their managers are equally good or sympathetic towards new businesses. The great advantage that the local manager ideally has over people at head office is that he knows local conditions and can advise you discreetly on trading conditions in the neighbourhood. He may even, in due course, pass your name on to customers who are looking for a service such as you are providing.

How your local bank manager can help

The bank manager will want to know the extent of your resources if you need to borrow money. He will need a cash flow projection, showing how much money you have coming in and going out for a twelve-month period at least, so that he can decide on the best method of funding you – and indeed to make a judgement on whether the franchise is likely to be a good investment from both your point of view and that of the bank. Again, he will not be able to advise you on whether this or that franchise is a good idea as such. As with any business decision, this ultimately boils down to personal judgement and homework, such as talking to other franchisees and checking the sort of points listed in previous chapters.

Your accountant

The preparation of a case to the bank for a loan or overdraft facilities – we will deal with sources of finance in more detail in Section 7 – is a step with which a good many franchisors will assist you. However, it is still highly desirable that you should get your own accountant to evaluate the franchisor's figures, as well as to conduct the necessary searches into the viability of the operation as a whole.

Your accountant should advise on the kind of company to set up

You will also need an accountant's advice on the best kind of business entity to set up. The usual thing is to establish the business as a limited company which has the effect, should things go terribly wrong, of limiting your liability to the issued share capital and assets of the company. However when a loan or overdraft facilities have been raised, these are usually subject to *personal* guarantees which override the limited liability of the company itself. Tax rulings in recent budgets have made forming a company less attractive in certain circumstances than remaining as a sole trader, personally liable for any trading debts incurred. Which form is chosen depends somewhat on the nature of the business involved. If you are incurring sizeable liabilities, as in the case of a retail outlet buying goods on credit, a limited company may well be the best way. With a job franchise it will probably pay you to be a sole trader.

The accountant will also advise you on what books and records to keep and if you do not want to do this yourself, he will probably recommend a book-keeper who can do this for you. In fact, there are even franchised accounting services which cater to small businesses. It may be a good idea to use such a service for routine advice and to go to a firm of qualified chartered accountants when you need more sophisticated or specialised information; for instance, on lessening your tax burden. An accountant will charge you around £50 an hour – so only use them for advice that is worth that kind of money!

Solicitors

Similar fees are charged by solicitors who can undertake some of the services offered by accountants, such as forming a company – though they will usually be less qualified to advise you on the pros and cons of this from a tax point of view.

Get a solicitor to vet the contract

The real value of a solicitor at this stage is to vet the franchise contract and any leases that go with it. You will greatly simplify his task by having a clear idea yourself beforehand of the sort of things you want to know. These are discussed in Section 6. Your solicitor should also advise you on any planning consents you need from the local authority.

If you are going into a franchise with a partner, you should get your solicitor to draw up a partnership agreement. The terms are fairly standard and cover points like how decisions are to be made and what happens if, for whatever reason, the partnership is dissolved.

Insurance

Does the policy cover everything? Usually the franchisor will arrange for this, either directly or indirectly but you should also get competitive quotes from a broker. You will need insurance of premises, contents, employer's and public liability and for any risks likely to arise from the nature of the franchise activity. Here again, the terms are fairly standard but it is important to read the policy to make sure that it covers.

CHECKLIST 7

Checking out the professional advisers

	✓ Yes	✓ No
1. If you are using a franchise adviser, have you asked him whether he has any connection with any of the firms he is recommending?	☐	☐
2. Have you spoken to other franchisees he has advised?	☐	☐
3. Have you prepared cash flow forecasts, profit and loss accounts and a business plan for the bank?	☐	☐
4. Have you made a proper assessment of your own resources and set a limit on what you can afford to lose?	☐	☐
5. Have you taken advice on whether it is best to form a company or operate as a sole trader?	☐	☐
6. If you have a partner, have you had a partnership agreement drawn up?	☐	☐
7. Have you taken steps to get full insurance cover? If the franchisor is supplying this, have you shown his proposal to your accountant or solicitor?	☐	☐

CHECKLIST 7

Checking out the professional advisers

Yes

No

Section 6

What to look for in the franchise contract

The legal side of the franchising contract can be very complex. This section takes you through the key issues you need to consider before you sign on the dotted line.

When you sign the franchise contract you will be making an even bigger commitment, all told, than when you bought your first house. In fact it might be compared to buying a house and getting married all at once because you are not only putting down a lot of money in relation to your resources (this also applies to the less expensive "job" franchises because these tend to be taken up by those with less capital) but you are also determining the course of your life for as long as the contract has to run.

Don't be pressurised into signing up

The first thing to be aware of, therefore, is the franchisor who tries to persuade you to sign up without giving the matter due thought. Although contracts based on having a pen thrust in your hand and asked to "sign here" are unenforceable without a cooling off period if the negotiations are taking place in your own home, you would be held to your word if it happened at the franchisor's premises. If you were actually to pay the fee in full you would not get your money back unless the sale was in some way fraudulent. No reputable franchisor would resort to such practices, but some of the cowboys have been known to put pressure on naive purchasers: for example, by indicating that another person is interested in the same franchise so that a quick decision is needed. Suggesting that the fee is about to go up and that you can save yourself a lot of money by signing "by Monday morning" is another dodge to be aware of.

But even when you are dealing with an established franchise you need to be clear what you are letting yourself in for and this is what the contract lays down. It sets out what you have to do and what the franchisor undertakes to do over the period for which the contract runs. It says how and when payment is to be made and it sets out the conditions under which the agreement can be terminated. Finally it tells you what conditions you have to observe if you want to sell the franchise.

There are now standard legal contracts for franchising – the principles are the same, but each one is a bit different. As well as reading the document yourself you should get a solicitor's comments on it. Of course, that solicitor should be your agent, not one suggested by the franchisor.

The purchase agreement

Is your deposit returnable?

The more expensive franchises such as shops and restaurants, need premises – and these are often not immediately available. Generally speaking the franchisor is responsible for finding the site; or at the very least, devoting a lot of time to helping you find it, checking it out for suitability, clearing legal permissions for its use and negotiating the sale or lease of the premises with their owners. Obviously the franchisor wants to have some sort of assurance that, subject to a suitable site being found, you will go ahead with the next step, which is to sign the actual franchise agreement. That assurance is incorporated in the Purchase Agreement which simply provides for you to pay a part of the franchise fee as a deposit to the franchisor's solicitors as a token of your serious intention to do so. If the franchisor then fails to find a suitable site within a reasonable period of time – and what those conditions mean ought to be defined to your satisfaction – the money you have paid in should be returned to you. Equally, if you change your mind or reject the site for no good reason, then you lose your deposit.

The franchise agreement

The franchise agreement will have been drawn up by the franchisor's solicitors and will be written in legal language which is not always easy for the lay person to follow. The object of this is not to confuse you, but rather to describe the various clauses that are being agreed in terms that are precise in law, should a dispute arise. Plain English does not always do this. The word "they" for instance can leave room for doubt about which party to the agreement is being referred to in a phrase like "They undertake to carry out local advertising."

Are you happy that all points are covered in the contract?

Many forms of agreement have the subject matter of groups of what can be long, involved clauses written into the margin; or they may group clauses together under some such heading as TERMINATION or FRANCHISEE'S OBLIGATIONS. If your contract does not have such headings or you cannot understand the ones that are there, make your own list of the points you think should be covered.

We have shown in Section 4 how to check on "What you should get for your money" in broad terms. The agreement deals more specifically with the relationship between you and the franchisor. It should therefore set out:

● The nature and name of the activity being franchised

● The franchise territory and how it is to be protected

● How long the agreement has to run

● The initial fee and continuing royalty

● What the franchisor agrees to do

● What the franchisee's obligations are

- The conditions under which the franchisee may sell or assign the business

- What happens at the end of the contract or how it can be terminated by either party

The nature and name of activity

In general all that these clauses do is to describe the product, service or process and guarantee that the franchisor is not "selling the Forth Bridge" – i.e. that he has the right to negotiate them and all the trade marks and specifications that may be involved. Be certain that what is set out in writing, actually corresponds to what you have been told verbally. Make sure nothing has been either added or omitted.

The franchise territory

The duration of the agreement

- Normally it should last for at least five years with an option to renew at the end of that time on the same terms; ideally without a further fee or at least on a basis to be mutually agreed well beforehand. Otherwise there is a chance, especially when you have taken on one of the less established franchises, that the franchisor will benefit unduly from the risk you have taken.

- Looking at the length of the lease, you should take into account that the period should be long enough to enable you to get back your start-up costs, plus a reasonable return on your investment and a living for yourself.

- If there are leased premises involved for which the lease runs longer than the duration of the franchise – or if you own the freehold – what restrictions are being placed on you to trade from here in another capacity if you want to terminate the franchise? The franchisor is within his rights in preventing you from immediately opening a competing activity from the same address. Generally he will say that you cannot do this for a period of time like 12-18 months.

- Check the lease to see whether you have an obligation to

make repairs at the end of the agreement. This can be very expensive.

How exclusive is exclusive

Some franchises use the term "exclusive" territory and this is then generally shown on an accompanying map. However "exclusive" agreements have to be registered with the Office of Fair Trading by the franchisor and because the OFT often imposes all kinds of restrictions on them many franchisors now talk of "privileged" territories. You obviously have to establish what anything short of exclusivity means. For example:

● How close is the next franchise at present?

● What are the franchisor's future plans for opening up outlets in the vicinity?

● Would he consult with you on such plans?

But whatever the basis it is vital to establish whether there has been a proper evaluation of the area you have been allotted to justify whatever claims are made about the revenue projected by the franchisor.

Franchise fees

The initial fee and continuing royalty

The franchise fee is quite distinct from the overall start-up costs of equipment, stock, shopfitting and so forth. It is paid to the franchisor to cover his costs in setting up the franchise – broadly in acquiring the know-how, piloting it, setting up the mechanisms and writing the manual. It is not, impartial advisers like the banks maintain, supposed to be a source of profit in itself and for that reason they suggest that the franchisor's initial fee should not exceed 10%-15% of the overall start-up costs. It can run a little higher in the case of the cheaper job franchises, but be on your guard much over that figure even if the royalty is low after that.

The normal royalty is in the region of 7½%-12½%, based on sales turnover, net of VAT. The points to check are:

● Are there any hidden extras, like an obligation to buy, possibly at uncompetitive rates, from sources nominated by the franchisor? There is nothing wrong with getting the advantages of bulk buying that often come with being a member of a group of franchisees, even if the franchisor makes a good profit for himself – but you should be free to find alternatives if the rates are not competitive.

● How often is payment due? Some franchisors insist on weekly royalties – great for their cash flow, bad for yours.

● Are there any minimum payments laid down, irrespective of turnover achieved? These are generally regarded as bad news and it is not a practice normally followed by reputable franchisors.

The franchisor's obligations

● A major source of dispute between franchisors and franchisees is when the latter feel they are paying substantial sums in royalties without getting very much in return. The way to protect yourself is to be sure that the contract does not allow this to happen.

● There should be proper training on all operational aspects. A clue here would be how much of the start-up costs are attributed to training. One franchise now on offer allocates £100 for accommodation during training. That implies that only about a week is being set aside for this all-important process.

Do the franchisor's promises match your needs?

● All franchises offer an operating manual of some sort. But are there free and regular updates?
The franchisor should provide assistance during the start-up period with legal as well as operational matters. Beyond that there should be help and back-up with specific problems, available promptly and free if the problems are related to snags within the franchise itself.

● Part of the royalty is usually devoted to advertising the franchise. The question to be resolved is how much of this is national and how much local and therefore specific to your franchise.

The franchisee's obligations

Since the shortcomings of any one outlet reflects badly on all the others, the franchisee's obligations are largely those related to following and protecting the business format in the way prescribed by the operating manual. The questions to consider therefore are whether these are reasonable and in line with what you had been given to understand verbally.

● You will be asked to follow the franchisor's directions on anything from the fitting out of the premises and the livery of your van to the graphics on your office stationery. Are these costs fully provided for in the start-up figures you have been given? Could they be a "hidden extra"?

Can you meet your part of the bargain?

● Agreeing to back the franchisor's promotional campaign may involve you in publicity costs that do not benefit you directly; or they may push up turnover (on which you pay your royalty) at the expense of profits. Try to limit such commitments.

● The contract may specify that you and all those associated with you devote your full time to running the franchise. Fair enough, you might say – but it can carry a hidden sting. It may make it difficult for you to set up as a limited company because all the directors would be bound by such a clause.

In the same connection it is worth checking that opening hours laid down by the franchisor accord with normal working practices. The income projected might not look so good if you find you have to work an 80-hour week to achieve it!

● Are there any irksome clauses? Agreeing to produce

detailed financial break-downs once a week might be something you will soon come to regret.

The conditions for selling or assigning the business

The right to do this is crucial and agreements which limit it should be looked on with suspicion.

- Reasonably, the franchisor can ask for first refusal, if you want to sell, at a market rate to be independently agreed; or he can ask to approve the purchaser since obviously the success of the franchise depends on the people operating each outlet. The essential proviso is that approval shall not be "unreasonably withheld".

- It would be unreasonable if the franchisor was to demand some kind of transfer fee from either party to such a transaction or to insist on a higher royalty rate from the purchaser than that which you had paid. This would certainly affect the value of what you have to sell.

Termination

It may sound premature to be thinking about termination before you have even started out but the termination clauses are a very important part of the contract. They determine what happens to it when it has run its course and under what circumstances you may ask or be asked to give up the business before then. The most likely event, though, is that you want to go on with it, so the first thing to look for is whether you can renew the agreement on the same terms – or at least on acceptable ones.

Is there a way out if things go wrong?

- By the same token the conditions under which the franchisor can terminate or refuse to renew the agreement must be reasonable ones – failure on your part to observe key conditions after having been given due warning, for instance. They must not be tied to performance targets.

● If the franchisor terminates the contract he should agree to buy back any remaining assets at a price to be independently assessed.

● Generally there will be a clause preventing you from carrying on a similar business in competition should you decide to discontinue the franchise – even if the premises or the lease are your own. That is reasonable. What is not reasonable – and would be regarded by the courts as such – is "restraint of trade" whereby you are prevented from carrying on any business you choose after about 12-18 months from the end of the contract.

● You should be allowed to terminate on your own initiative, for whatever reason and without penalty other than the loss of your initial fee.

Remember   The key point to bear in mind in reading the franchise agreement throughout is that it is drawn up by the franchisor's solicitors and will tend to favour him, if anyone. Do not assume, therefore, that you will get the benefit of any doubt and sign nothing until you have clearly understood or had explained to you the significance of every clause.

CHECKLIST 8

Taking a magnifying glass to the small print

	✔ Yes	✔ No
1. Have you taken enough time to study the contract?	☐	☐
2. Have you discussed it with a solicitor and received a satisfactory explanation of clauses you did not understand?	☐	☐
3. Does what the contract say agree with what the franchisor has told you?	☐	☐
4. Does it run for long enough to enable you to make a profit on your investment?	☐	☐
5. Are the initial fees and royalties reasonable in relation to what you now know?	☐	☐
6. Are there any clauses that you think you might find irksome and want to challenge before you sign?	☐	☐
7. Is the operating manual clear, easy to follow and regularly updated?	☐	☐
8. Are you free to sell the business and are any conditions the franchisor imposes reasonable?	☐	☐
9. Are the conditions under which the franchisor has the right to terminate reasonable?	☐	☐
10. Can you terminate without penalty if necessary?	☐	☐

Section 7

Raising the money

Raising finance for a good franchise is generally easier than raising cash for an untried business. But there are still ropes to learn. This section explains how to approach sources of finance, what they will expect of you and what you should expect of them.

Until fairly recently raising money was a major obstacle for anyone starting a small business of any kind. Finance generally had to be found by:

Selling assets, such as antiques, your car or your house

Selling an existing house at a profit and buying a new one with a higher mortgage

Taking out a second mortgage at high rates of interest because of the increased risk to the mortgagor.

All these options are still available but the banks now offer a number of more attractive alternatives. Indeed one could go so far as to say that if your application for funds is turned down by them – and you need not confine your approaches to your own bank, though they would be your best bet in the first instance – you should think twice about resorting to other sources of finance. The banks are not infallible, but they have a lot of experience in assessing lending risks, because essentially they make money by lending it out. If they think the deal you are putting to them is a bad risk, there are two possibilities: either they are not happy about the franchise or the people running it or you have not presented your case convincingly.

Banks and the franchisors

The franchisor should help draw up the business plan to the bank

Barclays and the Natwest both have franchising departments and a number of major franchisors have cleared their schemes with them. That does not by any means guarantee that you will get a loan if you take up one of those franchises – but it will obviously improve your chances. Such franchisors will, in fact, often help you to present your case to your local bank manager. Other franchisors are less well-known and there the bank will look at the contract and the revenue forecasts and decide whether the first is fair and the second, convincing. The banks, it should be noted, will seldom express an outright opinion about a franchise because of the fear of libel, but they will generally give you fairly unambiguous hints if they don't like the look of a particular proposition.

● Beware of franchisors who produce a non-committal letter of encouragement from some local branch manager as a sign of general approval. Its value is at best dubious.

Putting the case to the bank

The essence of putting your case to the bank – or indeed to any type of lender – is to put yourself in their shoes and figure out what you would want to know in the circumstances. In the case of the bank this is reassurance that:

What the bank is looking for

● Their money will be reasonably secure and covered by personal guarantees or assets like shares of quoted companies deposited with the bank.

● You have enough cash coming through to enable you to repay the loan and interest on a regular basis.

● The business will provide you with a living wage and a reasonable return on the capital you are putting in yourself.

An established franchise should have been shown to fill these conditions, which is why they are nowadays looked on quite favourably by the banks. In the first instance though, the bank will want to know how much money you yourself are putting in, whether this is enough and whether the bank's lending policy applied to your case will in fact be sufficient to make good any shortfall.

● Make a list of all your assets, separating cash and those that are immediately realisable like shares, from those that are more difficult or painful to turn into money: insurance policies, your home, personal possessions and so forth.

● Make a list of all your liabilities, again separating ones that you have to meet in the short term from longer term ones like the mortgage.

● By subtracting short term liabilities from short term assets you will get an idea of how much money you have immediately available. The longer term ones indicate what you could raise at a pinch.

The bank will lend you money on a basis usually ranging from 35%-70% of your requirements. What these are, depends firstly on your start-up costs – and the franchisor must be absolutely truthful about these – and secondly on the cash flow forecast.

The latter is a simple calculation in which you subtract, month by month and usually over a twelve-month period, all the outgoings the business has each month from the cash you started with at the beginning of the month plus all the receipts during that month. The cash you need should be enough to cover your worst deficit month. (A worked example and a full explanation of all this is given in *Working for Yourself,* The Daily Telegraph Guide to Self-Employment, published by Kogan Page.)

Meeting the bank's criteria

What the bank manager will want to see regularly

Apart from risking the money you put in right away you will also be asked to protect the bank's risk. They will ask you for a personal guarantee that you will reimburse them if things should go terribly wrong, and this could be covered by long term assets like your house. In practice, though, you will be ill-advised to over-extend yourself by putting every last available penny into your business and leaving no margin for disaster. Yes, fortunes have been made by people who did that, but more people have been reduced to penury by over-reaching themselves.

Finally the bank will want to be reasonably sure that the business is going to be profitable. Profitability is not the same thing as cash flow which is concerned with checking that there is enough cash coming in to pay the bills. Profitability is shown in the profit and loss account which is a set of figures showing total sales revenue less all costs over a given period. The franchisor will usually have prepared a specimen profit and loss account for the first year of operations, but this needs to be checked by your accountant. An inexperienced or less reputable franchisor could understate or even omit some costs in order to make the profit picture look rosier.

Types of loan

Apart from assessing whether you are a good risk and how much you need, the bank manager will also have to sort out what type of loan is best in the circumstances.

Overdrafts

● The most straightforward kind and the one with which most people are already familiar is simply an overdraft facility up to a certain level. The *advantage* is that you only pay interest on the actual amount of the overdraft you are using – i.e. not on the total amount of the facility. The *disadvantages* are firstly that interest rates on overdrafts are not fixed but vary with the bank rate, which makes planning difficult; and secondly that overdrafts are theoretically repayable on demand. They should not be used to finance long-term requirements, like those involved in equipment and start-up costs.

Term loans ● These extend over a period of time in which the capital has to be repaid as well as the interest. Interest payments can be made at a fixed rate – usually about 3% above the going bank rate at the time the loan was made. The problem here is that if the rate falls sharply thereafter – and it has been as high as 17% during the recession – you are going to be stuck with that burden for the duration of the loan.

Term loans are obviously suitable to finance expenditures which can only be recovered over a period of time and the banks have set up a number of schemes which are particularly geared to small businesses.

If they feel uncertain about taking the risk themselves they may try to help you get a Government Loan Guarantee. These are available for up to £75,000 and are administered by the banks. The taxpayer in effect acts as guarantor for up to 80% of the money the bank advises. The *disadvantage* however, is that they carry a higher rate of interest than an ordinary bank loan.

Leasing and lease purchase ● Many of the banks have subsidiaries or related companies who are involved in leasing and hire purchase of equipment and vehicles; or you can shop around for competitive rates. Interest rates are also higher than those you get if you borrow money direct but the big *advantages* of leasing are firstly that you do not pay the full cost of the equipment immediately – only a deposit as with ordinary domestic HP; secondly that you have more of a hold over the supplier of unsatisfactory leased equipment than you do when you make an outright purchase. The *disadvantages* generally lie in the small print. You may find that the rate of interest is inordinately high. Nowadays, by the way, that has to be stated in writing by the supplier.

The main difference between leasing and hire purchase is that in the latter case you have the option to become the owner of the equipment after a certain number of payments have been made. However, leases can also be extended, often very cheaply, when they come to the end of their normal term.

Private loans

● You may have friends or relatives who are prepared to lend you money, though if the banks are not willing to do so it might be unfair to ask those who are less able to afford it to take the risk. However the circumstances may be that a private loan is available at preferential rates, or to make good the shortfall in your own resources.

Private loans can be a rich source of misunderstanding, so it is advisable to get a solicitor to draw up a proper document setting out the amount and period of the loan, the rate of interest and at what intervals interest payments and capital repayments are due. However – and this is where problems tend to arise – lenders must be quite clear that making a loan does not entitle them to a say in the running of the business, nor to a share of the profits unless the agreement you have made expressly says so.

A share in the profits could, however, come into it if you were forming a limited company and the loan was tied to the lender being given the opportunity to acquire shares; or alternatively if what you were raising was not a loan at all, but capital by means of selling shares. The latter option has been made quite attractive in tax terms by the government's Business Expansion Scheme which allows lenders personally unconnected with the directors to set off investments in small unquoted companies against income tax.

The *disadvantage* of offering shares is that the shareholders are entitled to a proportion of the profits directly related to the percentage of their shareholding.

Financing your business from normal trading

● A source of finance that is often overlooked is that you can generate a surprising amount of cash simply by taking the maximum amount of credit suppliers will give you, while keeping a tight control over your debtors. In any business, the more cash sales you make and the more credit purchases you transact, the better. At normal interest rates, taking full advantage of the 30 days you are generally given to pay bills will be worth at least an extra 1% a month on money that you owe.

CHECKLIST 9

Is the funding right?

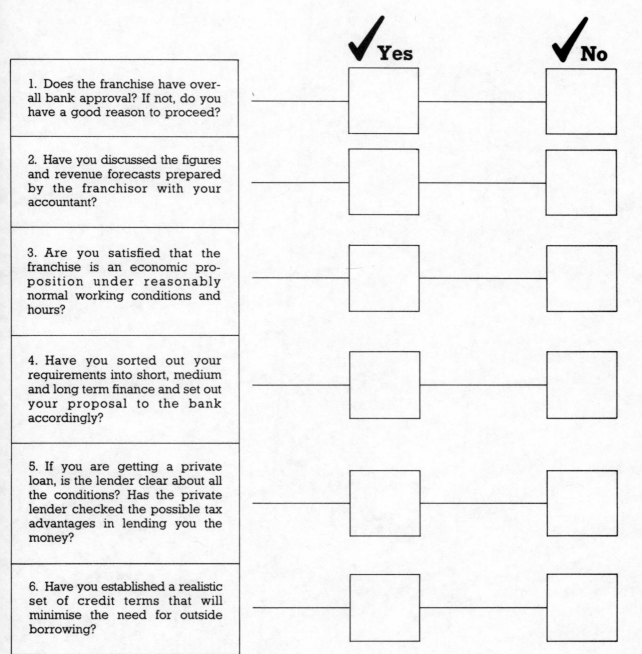

✓ **Yes** ✓ **No**

1. Does the franchise have over-all bank approval? If not, do you have a good reason to proceed?

2. Have you discussed the figures and revenue forecasts prepared by the franchisor with your accountant?

3. Are you satisfied that the franchise is an economic pro-position under reasonably normal working conditions and hours?

4. Have you sorted out your requirements into short, medium and long term finance and set out your proposal to the bank accordingly?

5. If you are getting a private loan, is the lender clear about all the conditions? Has the private lender checked the possible tax advantages in lending you the money?

6. Have you established a realistic set of credit terms that will minimise the need for outside borrowing?

Case History 4

Money in the drains

Dyno-rod was started in the early sixties and like a lot of good business ideas it began with one man discovering that something he needed was a) not available and b) needed by a lot of other people as well. That man was Jim Zockoll. He was a London-based PanAm pilot and when the drains in his Surrey house seized up, he found he couldn't get a plumber to come and fix them. He tried looking through the Yellow Pages – but found there was no such publication in the UK. On his next transatlantic flight he tried to get the rights to publish a British version of this American invention, but he found that Thomson Newspapers had pipped him to the post. So he did the next best thing – he bought the rights to an American drain clearing machine and set up a part-time business with it. It was an immediate success and he started getting enquiries from all over the country. Since he wanted to go on being a pilot and couldn't do that as well as run a UK wide business, he decided to franchise his system, which he called Dyno-rod. At that time hardly anyone in Britain even knew what franchising was and Jim sold his first franchises for as little as £500. Today a Dyno-rod franchise would set you back about £150,000 and you would have to buy one from an existing franchisee, because all the 44 UK Dyno-rod franchises are taken up. What Jim is now doing is buying them back from the franchisees when they want to sell out – at full market rates, of course. Then he is breaking them up into smaller units as one man van operations. They still keep the name and do the same sort of things, but the cost of an OMV franchise is only £15,000, which is much more within the price range an ordinary individual can afford. £3000 of that is Dyno-rod's initial fee and the rest is made up of equipment and the van. There is a 20% royalty. Both that and the fee are high in comparison to other franchises, but then Dyno-rod is an established name and has been successful for 20 years.

At any rate Peter Curtis, a partner in the Dyno-rod franchise in south London thinks it's worth it. "The name alone is a guarantee that you will get the business," he says. "Dyno-rod came out well in comparison to several other drain clearing services in a recent 'Which' survey, but that's only what the customer sees. The back-up from the franchisor is first rate. They produce excellent literature both for sales promotion and to keep us up on technical developments."

The latter is important because about 75% of Dyno-rod's business is from industrial and commercial work and that is where the big money is. "Industrial processes involve a lot of ducts and pipes which can get clogged up with all kinds of deposits, ranging from the solid to the sticky," Curtis says. "And there's also a lot of local authority work – clearing the drains in school kitchens, for instance. Down on the south coast, there is a franchisee who does a lot of marine contracts. He was involved in re-fitting some of the ships that were converted to military use during the Falklands war."

Naturally this involves some very pricey equipment. "The basic Dyno-rod tool is very simple", he says. "It's a revolving cable plugged to a machine and there are various attachments for crushing, cutting, scraping and so forth. That costs about £4500. But for tougher jobs you would need a high speed water jet which can cut through anything. They run to about £15,000 and we have four of them. But then we're a sizeable business with four operators – some franchisees call them engineers and in fact we have had graduates working for us – and a salesman calling on customers throughout our exclusive territory." There are some tools that are expensive even for a business of that size; for instance, there is now a TV monitor attached to a video which can be run along extensive underground systems to do surveys – another aspect of Dyno-rod's service. "We don't often have to use that piece of equipment, but there's a good informal network among the franchisees which is sponsored by the franchisor, through our newsheet and through regular meetings at the head office in Surbiton. So when we need a piece of expensive equipment on a one-off basis we borrow or hire from each other."

Although it all sounds very technical both Curtis and Dyno-rod's headquarter staff say that you don't need any technical qualifications to start with. There is a three week intensive training programme at the beginning and it's tailored to people with a wide variety of backgrounds. "We do have some engineers and ex-plumbers among our franchisees, but they also include an accountant, an ex-advertising executive and several people who were formally in general management", says Russ Taylor, Dyno-rod's marketing director. "Previous knowledge is obviously useful – but it can also be a handicap if you've got into a very set way of doing things. Sometimes clearing an obstacle can be a matter of applying ingenuity; you might have to rig up a special device as happened recently when we had to clear an obstruction in a 700 ft high pipe on an oil rig."

There is always the expertise at the head office to fall back on, based on feedback from other franchisees. In fact one of the advantages of an established franchise like Dyno-rod is that you are independent, but not on your own. That also applies to advice on legal and financial matters.

According to Russ Taylor, a full Dyno-rod franchisee can make an income in the £30,000 a year plus range – even after employing the necessary staff and paying a high 20% royalty due monthly. The income from the OMV operations is obviously less, but the way to get started is the same. "We don't take anybody," he says. "Not even anybody who's got the money! In fact our franchisees have no difficulty getting finance of up to 75% from the banks. That is because the banks know that we have vetted them thoroughly first. What happens is that when people write in, we have a series of discussions with them to assess their suitability and financial status – you still have to be able to find a quarter of the startup costs yourself. If we think they're right we ask them to pay a deposit which is subject to the contract. You can change your mind right up to contract signature, though we might withhold some of the money – not more than £250 – to defray our costs up to that point. We do have costs because we help intending franchisees prepare their case to the bank. We provide cash flows, revenue forecasts, a business plan in consultation with the franchisee – all the sort of information the bank manager needs to make his decision."

The OMV franchise is identical to the full Dyno-rod one with the exception that it doesn't provide an "exclusive" territory. There are, however, privileged areas in which other franchisees would be discouraged from seeking customers. It's fair to say that Peter Curtis is not entirely happy about the advent of OMV operators carrying the Dyno-rod name. "I accept the fact that it may be the only way in which new people can come in unless they have a lot of money to start with, but of course we do depend on Dyno-rod's as they have been in the past. A successful franchise depends very much on each franchisee being up to the mark. One bad operator can reflect on the whole chain. On the other hand, Dyno-rod has had an excellent record in that respect so far – and I see no reason why that should change. However, changes in the method of operation like the OMV concept would be something to beware of if you're signing up with one of the less established franchises.

Section 8

Monitoring your progress

In this section we show some of the methods you can use to make sure your business is on the right track. What information should you be supplying the bank? And what do you need to know about the finances of your business on a week to week or month to month basis? How can you tell if you are really doing well or badly?

In the previous section we listed the criteria the banks apply when deciding whether they will lend you money:

● That you are likely to do sufficiently well to repay the loan and the interest in a regular fashion.

● That you are likely to make a reasonable living for yourself while getting an adequate return on the money you yourself have invested (don't forget you could have invested it in a fixed term deposit account and got a substantial return on it without any risk).

This is not just a one-off exercise but a process of continuing appraisal. That is how you should look at it even if you have funded the franchise without having to get a loan at all; and certainly if you have borrowed money from a bank, it will want to monitor progress at regular intervals.

What are the crucial indicators they will want to examine?

Cash flow

The bank manager will not be an expert in your particular form of business, so in the first instance he will have to rely on the revenue and expenditure figures you and the franchisor have produced – though he may point out omissions or guesstimates that he knows to be out in the light of his knowledge of local trading conditions. Very soon, though, he will want to see *actual* figures and compare these with the forecast. These may indicate that you will need to cut back certain items of expenditure or achieve a higher volume of sales. One of the disadvantages of franchising is that when the franchisor has laid down a very specific method of operating in his manual, it may be difficult to make such adjustments – hence, once again, the importance of checking the contract in the first place.

Break-even levels

Some franchises, particularly the "job" variety base their revenue forecasts on your reaching a certain level of transactions: – so many offices cleaned per day, so many double glazing units installed per week, or whatever. Here the crucial point is how many transactions you have to make to break even over a given period – taking into account *all* your costs, including your own wage. Some franchisors omit this last consideration and make it easier to reach a genuine break even figure than is really the case. You can easily check their sums beforehand for yourself.

Supposing you had been given a projected revenue of £16,000 a year, based on £20 per call. That means 800 calls a year and if you worked a 50-week year that would mean 16 calls a week. In the first place you have to decide whether this is a realistic call rate. Some less reputable job franchisors produce information on call rates which seems to be deliberately misleading. One circulating at present gives a "record figure" for one week which suggests that the much lower average figure is easy to achieve. Without knowing in what circumstances that record was achieved (a one-off rush job for one big customer?) and for how long it was sustained, figures like that are at best meaningless.

Having embarked on a job franchise, you have to check your progress by seeing whether you are achieving the weekly work rates that are necessary to reach the anticipated revenue levels.

Business ratios

Choose the right business ratios for your business and check them regularly

A profit and loss account for any given period – very simply a set of accounts in which all your costs are set out and subtracted from all your revenues – will also give you other information. For instance, if you are maintaining credit accounts, the amount of money owed to you currently, divided by sales over the period covered by the profit and loss account and multiplied by the number of days in a year will give you an accurate indication of whether your terms of supply are being observed, e.g.

$$\frac{\text{Debtors} \quad (\text{say } £1000)}{\text{Sales} \quad\;\; (\text{say } £10,000)}$$
$$\times\ 365$$

= 36.5 is the average number of days debtors are taking to settle

More important, from the point of view of whether the funds in the business are being profitably employed is the ratio between the actual profit and the amount of money invested in cash, stocks and other assets. This is usually an exercise taken over the course of a year, but you can use the profit over a shorter period, to estimate the long term trend.

$$\frac{\text{Profit} \quad (\text{say } £1000)}{\text{Funds} \quad (\text{say } £10,000)}$$
$$\times\ 100 = 10\% \text{ return on funds}$$

In the case of a retail franchise an important ratio is the relationship between the value of sales and the cost of stocks. This will indicate how quickly the stock is turning over.

$$\frac{\text{Sales} \quad (\text{say } £10,000)}{\text{Stock} \quad (\text{say } £2500)}$$

$= 4 \times$ stock turnover

In general the lower the stock figure is in relation to sales, the better the business is doing, assuming another ratio is in order.

$$\frac{\text{Cost of Sales}}{\text{Sales}}$$

$\times 100 = \%$age margin

There are in fact, a great many ratios that can be applied but they are obviously not equally relevant to every type of business. A franchise doing all of its trade in cash would not be interested in debtor days, nor would a job franchise with no stocks (also known as inventory, a term more widely used in the USA) be greatly concerned with the stock to sales ratios. The point to discuss with your bank or your accountant is which the relevant ones are and also what the average standards are for your type of business; for instance, how many times a year a DIY shop should turn over its stock. The average annual rate of stock turn can vary tremendously between types of business. Marks & Spencer aims for 18 times, for example, while a garden centre may achieve only 3 or 4.

If you fall behind plan, discuss it with the franchisor – it's his problem, too!

What happens if you are not keeping up to these objectives? The problem with a franchise where things like opening hours or trading activities or territories are fixed is that you have less freedom of action than a totally independent operator who can increase his prices, stay open longer, stock more goods or look for customers further afield. However if you are falling short of your objectives it may be because the franchisor was over-optimistic about what could be achieved. It is in his interest as much as yours that you should succeed and you should get together with him to see how the problem can be solved: perhaps by tinkering with some aspect of the format – or even by the franchisor agreeing to accept a lower royalty until things get back on track!

CHECKLIST 10

Monitoring your progress

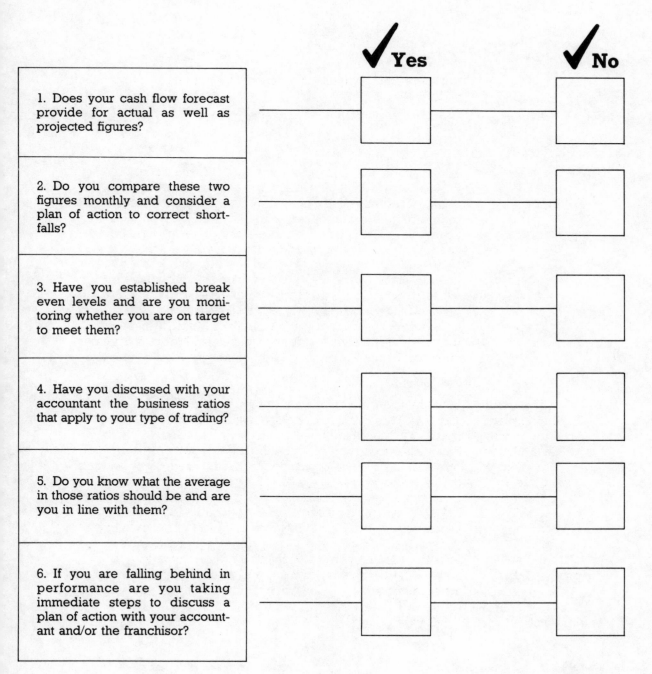

✔ **Yes**   ✔ **No**

1. Does your cash flow forecast provide for actual as well as projected figures?

2. Do you compare these two figures monthly and consider a plan of action to correct short-falls?

3. Have you established break even levels and are you monitoring whether you are on target to meet them?

4. Have you discussed with your accountant the business ratios that apply to your type of trading?

5. Do you know what the average in those ratios should be and are you in line with them?

6. If you are falling behind in performance are you taking immediate steps to discuss a plan of action with your accountant and/or the franchisor?

Section 9

Franchising your own business

In this final section, we look at franchising from the other side of the coin – the would-be franchisor. Not all successful business ideas are suitable for franchising, but those that are can provide substantial income without massive capital outlay.

The growing interest in franchising is not confined to people who want to become franchisees. There is also an increasing number of businesses who want to establish franchises – to become franchisors. Some are large companies, which would have no difficulty in financing branches of their own, but which feel that a franchisee would be more motivated. They also often consider that the franchisee ultimately produces a better return than company-employed branch managers. Other franchisors are smaller firms looking for ways of expanding without committing the capital and management time that is required for opening their own outlets.

Some big companies have nationally recognised names and products and some individual entrepreneurs with smaller companies have excellent ideas. However neither of these are enough in themselves to add up to a guarantee of franchiseability. So what characteristics do you look for in deciding whether your activity lends itself to expansion by means of business format franchising?

Characteristics of a franchiseable business

Is your
business
suitable?

A "unique" product or service is often considered vital because of the mystique created by such pioneers as Wimpy or Kentucky Fried Chicken, with their "secret recipes". But though some such feature is important it is not enough in itself. You also need

● A product or service that satisfies a continuing consumer demand. To be able to demonstrate to franchisees that they can get their start-up costs back in 3-4 years if they follow the format laid down.

● To have a format that is simple and rather mechanical to follow. A product or service that depends to a high degree on individual flair and skill is very difficult to franchise.

● A simple and memorable name.

● Uniform standards of quality and appearance for all outlets.

● To make sure beforehand that suitable premises in the right positions and with proper access are likely to be available within a price range that franchisees can afford.

● Administrative processes that can be kept simple.

● A strong enough financial position to provide adequate training and back-up services.

● To ensure that the franchise should either have a trade "secret" or patentable device; or that it should have some characteristics that can be marketed as being unique or virtually so – e.g. that all hamburgers are 100% pure meat.

● Support from a clearing bank for your scheme, so that prospective franchisees have a reasonable assurance of financial support.

Piloting the franchise

It takes time,
trial and error
to prove the
franchise
works

A lot of what it takes for a franchise to be a success can only be established by trial and error – and that has to be at the franchisor's cost, not the franchisee's. The British Franchise Association makes it a condition of membership that an operation has to be piloted for at least two years and it can be quite a costly process, both directly and in terms of management time. It is not a question of simply turning a branch into a franchise, and seeing whether it turns in a profit. It involves:

● Choosing an area and a site which will give you a fair picture of the market. Some franchisors, in fact, think that there should be at least two pilot operations in different locations.

● Testing equipment, staffing levels, services or products, opening hours, advertising and publicity policies to arrive at a profitable mix.

● Perfecting internal and external financial reporting procedures and defining key areas.

● Establishing costs so that pricing policies can be set or suggested. Setting out training procedures both for franchisees and for the franchisor's own staff in their trouble shooting roles.

● Preparing and testing the blueprint or operating manual.

● Experienced franchisors suggest that the pilot operation can only be a true test if it is actually run as a proper franchise; i.e. it should be expected to pay a notional royalty and be on track to yield the results that the franchisor will be setting out in the prospectus when he starts marketing the operation. As an inducement to the manager of the pilot outlet he is sometimes given the option to become the actual franchisee at the end of this phase, either without paying a fee or at a greatly reduced one.

At the same time the franchisor must establish some idea of what all the costs are. It is on this that you base the income levels you require from the initial fee, the continuing royalty and the profits from sales of goods and equipment to the franchisee – always bearing in mind, of course, that the start-up costs can only be recovered over a period of time. If you overload the front end fee or the royalty, you will not get franchisees – or at least, not the right ones.

Choosing franchisees

The success of a franchise depends quite as much on the franchisees as on the quality of the product or service. Nearly all franchisors, it emerged at a recent seminar, feel that their first franchisees were poor choices. There is a temptation to take their money and get the show on the road, often combined with lack of experience in making the right choices. The main factors to take into account are:

What to look for in potential franchisees

● **Character and motivation** – Franchisees have to be fully committed to the work and all it entails. However, very independent-minded individuals do not make good franchisees. A good number two, it is said, is best suited to this form of trading.

● **A supportive family** – some franchisors like to meet the spouse as well.

● **Experience** – though administrative and sales experience is considered by many to be more important than direct experience of the type of business involved.

● **Financial soundness** – The ideal franchisee is someone who is using some of his own money and borrowing the rest. This increases his motivation. It also acts as a double check because he has to satisfy the bank that he is a good risk.

Questions franchisees are likely to ask

A good franchisee will have checked you out carefully before committing himself. Very likely he will have taken advice from his solicitor, his accountant and his bank manager. They will want him to be satisfied on the following points, many of which have been raised in earlier chapters.

● What is the issued capital of the company that owns the franchise?

● What is the size of your headquarters staff?

● Have you disclosed all sources of money you expect to earn from the franchise other than the fee and royalty?

● How well can you protect the franchise from competition?

● What constraints, if any, are there when the franchisee wants to sell the business?

● What are the conditions for renewing at the end of the contract?

● What happens if the franchisee finds he wants to terminate before the end of the contract period?

Some of these questions will actually be covered in the contract, but in so far as they are not, you should confirm anything you have told the franchisee in writing. Just as you are keen to sell the franchise – and may be tempted to gloss over some of its disadvantages in consequence – so the intending franchisee may be over-keen to buy and not to take in everything you say; or his memory may simply be at fault. Having it in writing may not prevent recrimination, but it does prevent litigation.

CHECKLIST 11

Can you franchise your business?

	Yes	No
1. Have you considered the pros and cons of franchising as compared to other ways of expanding your business?	☐	☐
2. Are your methods of operation and processes simple enough to be followed by an inexperienced person, given some training?	☐	☐
3. Have you identified the special features of your product or service that will give it the edge on competing ones?	☐	☐
4. Do you have a good simple name for the franchise?	☐	☐
5. Have you discussed with solicitors whether any part of your product or service can be patented or trade marked?	☐	☐
6. Have you piloted the franchise in a characteristic area for a reasonable period of time?	☐	☐
7. Is your sales literature to franchisees truthful in every respect? (You could be held liable for any mis-statement.)	☐	☐
8. Do you have a proper set of procedures for interviewing and vetting the suitability of potential franchisees and their financial status?	☐	☐
9. Are you prepared for all the questions the franchisee may ask about you and your business?	☐	☐

Case History 5

When a franchise is the answer

For many people, especially the newly redundant, a franchise may appear to be just the job. It combines day-to-day independence with expert back-up and advice should things go wrong. It has all the advantages of self-employment with fewer of the risks than if you are going it totally on your own.

Dixon Keir, 40, has been selling and installing franchised home security systems – an up market term for burglar alarms – since December 1982. He says: "One of the great selling points of a franchise is the feeling of independence. I go to a house, install the system and get a great sense of satisfaction that things work!"

He adds that though technical back-up is always available if a hitch occurs it may be many miles from the actual source of the problem. So if you are considering a franchise, you should ideally know something about the field you will be working in.

Familiar area

Mr Keir, who lives in Hamilton, Lancashire, took up his franchise with a company called Jessop Hall Home Security

Systems after seeing it advertised in *Executive Post*. His background in both production and maintenance engineering meant that he would be operating in a familiar area. "I got information on a lot of franchises. Most I discarded fairly quickly because I wasn't suited to them."

The Jessop Hall Home Security System is a relatively low cost installation which includes an external bell box, control panel, "personal attack button", pressure mat and anti-tamper device to protect it from burglar interference and a battery in case the mains electricity supply is cut off. Each franchise costs about £5500.

Franchisees are responsible for spotting prospective clients, visiting their premises to discuss their needs, and finally putting in the security system and providing any follow-up.

Another of Jessop Hall's 18 franchisees is 51 year old Bernard Taylor from Farnham in Surrey. Like Mr Keir he has an engineering background and was working as a sales engineer when redundancy struck and he was left high and dry without any lump sum payment at a vulnerable age. He says: "I was in a very difficult position. I looked at ways of earning my living on my own. Because I had received no redundancy payment I decided to raise cash on my house to take up the franchise. I was confident I could sell what they were offering provided a market really existed for it."

He set about doing his homework, both on Jessop Hall and the home security market. He comments: "Everywhere I went I was told that the alarm industry is one of today's growth areas. In fact, the more I looked, the more I was convinced."

When Dixon Keir took voluntary redundancy from British Steel last year he was given a redundancy payment. He had been mulling over the possibility of setting up on his own for some time; as a personnel manager with BSC, Mr Keir had been involved in a number of plant closures over the years. That accelerating programme opened his mind to the possibility that his own job might disappear in its turn, leaving him in an adverse jobs market.

Involve the family

He selected Jessop Hall as the front runner franchise choice and took his wife along to its Peterborough headquarters to look at the firm and its product. He stresses the need to involve the family, particularly your husband or wife, when deciding to go it alone. "The hours you may have to work can cause disruption to family life. You must be prepared to go out when needed, even if it's a Sunday or an evening."

There's an equally pressing reason for involving your partner – the need for someone to be on hand at home to deal with telephone queries when you're out or to man your stand at trade fairs if you're chatting to a potential client. If your family are at odds with you on this score, the chances of success will be considerably lessened.

We asked Mr Keir and Mr Taylor how their businesses had turned out for them. According to Mr Taylor: "It's early days yet and therefore a question of building the job up. Things tend to be patchy – I had a slack time in July and August – though I'm quite optimistic the business will expand over the next 12 months when I hope to take on at least one other person."

Mr Keir agrees about July and August. "People aren't worried about security systems then – they are more interested in spending money on holidays in Tenerife."

He adds that a franchise is not an easy way to make money. "It is less likely to fail than when you set up entirely on your own, though it's not guaranteed you'll succeed. It's necessary to go in with your eyes open. Talk to a good lawyer and a good accountant to ensure your franchise contract is what you want, that in itself will give you a flying start."

Reprinted by permission of Executive Post

DIRECTORY

Members and associates of the British Franchise Association

The British Franchise Association has about forty members and has been around for three years. Their member companies can account for about £280 million sales each year, and they are growing. Combined sales outlets have doubled from 2000 in 1979 to 4000 in 1981 and the member companies employ more than 20,000 people – a 24% increase since 1978.

Apollo Window Blinds Ltd., 79 Johnstone Avenue, Cardonald Industrial Estate, Glasgow, G52. Mr. James Watson, 041-810 3021. Retail Franchise – Supply all types of fashion window blinds and associated services.

Autopro, Swift Tools Ltd., Badminton Road Trading Est., Yate, Bristol, BS17 5JS. Mr. S.B. Parkin or Mr. N. Bradshaw, (0454) 314971 (Chipping Sodbury). Sale of Tools to the Garage Trade through Van Sale Distribution.

British School of Motoring Ltd., 102 Sydney Street, Chelsea, London SW3 6NJ. Mr. David Acheson, 01-351 2377. Driving Tuition.

Budget Rent-a-Car International Inc. International House, 85 Gt. North Road, Hatfield, Herts. AL9 5EF. Mr. Max McHardy, Hatfield 68266. National & International self-drive Car, Van & Truck rental service.

City Link Transport Holdings Ltd., 13/14 Ascot Road, Clockhouse Lane, Feltham, Middlesex, TW14 8QF. Mr. Robert Thomas, Ashford 43721. Same Day & Overnight Parcel-Delivery service.

Colour Counsellors Ltd., 187 New King's Road, Parson's Green, London SW6. Mrs. V. Stourton, 01-736 8326. Interior Decorating: colour catalogued samples of wallpapers, carpets & fabrics.

Cookmate Reject Kitchen Shop, Cookshop Supplies Ltd., Unit 5, Southern Road, Aylesbury, Bucks. Mr. Brian Howlett, Aylesbury 20695. Fast-selling kitchen gadgets, equipment, accessories & furniture in glass, china, metal, plastic & wood (retail).

Dinol (Car Care) UK Ltd., Commerce House, Stuart Street, Luton, Beds, LU1 5BY. Mr. K.S. Wilberg, Luton 413071. Vehicle rust-proofing, Sunroofs & other car-care services.

Dyno-Rod Ltd., The Zockoll Group, Zockoll House, 143 Maple Road, Surbiton, Surrey, KT6 4BJ. Mr. Vaughan, Thursby-Pelham 01-549 9711. Drain & Pipe cleaning service.

GKN Spa Ltd., Station Tower, Station Square, Coventry, CV1 2GR. Mr. John Ovens, Coventry 555491 (Code 0203). Service includes retailing of Motor Accessories & Replacement Parts.

Halford's Franchise, Halfords Ltd., George House, 121 High Street, Henley in Arden, Solihull, West Midlands, B95 5AU. Mr. Albert Lee, Henley in Arden (Code 05642) 3378. Retailing motor accessories, cycles, camping, caravanning & leisure goods. (Isle of Man, Channel Isl. and Ireland.)

Happy Eater Ltd.,* 30 Upper High Street, Epsom, Surrey, KT17 4QJ. Mr. Allen Jones, Epsom 25611. Restaurants.

Holiday Inns (UK) Inc., Windmill House, Windmill Road, Brentford, Middlesex, TW8 0QH. Mr. John Duncan, 01-568 8800. Hotels.

Home Tune Ltd., Home Tune House, Guildford Road, Effingham, Nr. Leatherhead, Surrey, KT24 5QS. Mr. Duncan Whitfield, Bookham 56656. Car-tuning service.

Kall-Kwik Printing, K K Printing (UK) Limited, Kall-Kwik House, Tennyson Rd., Hanwell, Middlesex, W7 1LH. Mr. M. Gerstenhaber, 01-840 3222. Quick Printing Centres offering comprehensive design, printing, finishing & photocopying services.

Kentucky Fried Chicken (GB) Ltd., Hawley Lane, Farnborough, Hants. Mr. Julien Fletcher, Farnborough (Hants), (0252) 516251. Fast Food.

Ladyline (Holdings) Ltd., Bank Chambers, 3 Cheshire Street, Market Drayton, Shropshire, TF9 1JN. Mr. J. Riordan, Market Drayton (0630) 2217. Retailing of Marine & Outdoor Leisure Products.

Phildar (UK) Ltd.,* 4 Gambrel Road, Westgate Industrial Estate, Northampton, NN5 5NF. Mr. John Shannon, Northampton (0604) 583111. Retailing of company's own products, namely knitting yarns, DIY products & accessories.

PizzaExpress Ltd., 29 Wardour Street, London W1V 3HB. Mr. Ian Neill, 01-437 7215. Pizzeria Restaurants.

Pizza Hut Inc. (UK branch), 149 Earl's Court Road, Kensington, London SW5. Mr. Peter Bassi, 01-370 6440. Family-oriented Restaurants.

Power-Rod Ltd., Lidgra House, 250 Kingsbury Road, London NW9. Mr. David Wheeler, 01-204 9018. Drain & Pipe-cleaning contractors.

(* denotes **"B.F.A. Associates"**)

Prontaprint Ltd., Executive Offices, Coniscliffe House, Darlington, DL3 7EX. Mr. Martin Richmond, Darlington (0325) 55391. Printing shops.

Pronuptia & Youngs (Franchise) Ltd., 70/78 York Way, King's Cross, London N1. Mr. Edward Young, 01-278 7722. Bridal attire retail shops: formal wear hire-service for men.

Safeclean International, D.G. Cook Ltd., Pound House, Upton, Didcot, Oxon, OX11 9JG. Mr. Desmond Cook, Blewbury (0235) 850387. Hand-cleaning of carpets & upholstery: curtain cleaning on site.

Scottish & Newcastle Inns Ltd., Abbey Brewery, 111 Holyrood Road, Edinburgh. Mr. Andrew James, 031-556 2591 (Extension 2887). Public Houses, Restaurants & Off-Licence Shops.

ServiceMaster Ltd., 50 Commercial Square, Freeman's Common, Leicester, LE2 7SR. Mr. Brian Smith, Leicester (0533) 548620. On site carpet, upholstery & curtain-cleaning; fire & flood restoration; carpet treatment & repairs.

Servowarm, Servotomic Ltd., 199 The Vale, Acton, London W3 7YY. Mr. Ted Brammer, 01-743 1244. Central Heating & Central Heating products.

Silver Shield Screens Ltd., 38-42 Holbrook Lane, Coventry, West Midlands. Mr. John Oliver, Coventry (0203) 661311. 24-hour mobile Windscreen Replacement service.

Spud-U-Like Ltd.,* 19a Coates Crescent, Edinburgh. Mr. Kim F. Culley, 031-226 4422/3. Fast Food Restaurants based on Baked Potatoes with large variety of fillings.

Steiner Products Ltd., The Broadway Cottages, Stanmore, Middlesex, HA7 4DU. Mr. J.G. Macaulay, 01-954 6121. Ladies & Mens Hairdressing & Beauty.

The **Coca Cola** Export Corporation, Pemberton House, Wright's Lane, London W8 5SN. Mr. John Marwood, 01-938 2131. Soft Drinks.

Thorntons, J.W. Thornton Ltd., Derwent Street, Belper, Derbyshire, DE5 1WP. Mr. R.E. Smith, Belper (077 382) 4181. Specialist Chocolate & Sugar Confectionery Retail.

Thuro-Clean Ltd.,* 65 Bondway, London SW8 1SJ. Mr. Ralph James, 01-582 6033. "In Home" cleaning of carpets, upholstery & curtains: carpet dyeing and soft-furnishings service after flood/fire.

TI/Midas Ltd., 332/336 Goldhawk Road, Hammersmith, London W6 0XF. Mr. Nicholas Greville, 01-741 1156. Retail exhaust-system replacement.

Mobiletuning Ltd., 16 The Market, Greenwich, London SE10 9HZ. Mr. A.R. Rowntree, 01-853 1520. Mobile car engine-tuning service.

Unipart Ltd., Unipart House, Garsington Road, Cowley, Oxford, OX4 2PG. Oxford (0865) 778966

Uticolor (Great Britain) Ltd., Sheraton House, 35 North Street, York, YO1 1JD. Mr. Eric Bottomley, York (0904) 37798. Repair, Recolouring & Restoration of Vinyl coverings.

Willie Wurst Inns, Cloverbest Restaurant Associates Ltd., Ingleside House, Hawarden Avenue, Douglas, Isle of Man. Mr. J. Stephen Murray, Douglas (0624) 21121. Retail sales of traditional German sausages.
Wimpy International Ltd., 214 Chiswick High Road, London W4 1PH. Mr. Tony Dutfield, 01-994 6454. Fast Food.